ESSENTIAL HORSE
Conformation

51 Checkpoints Before You Buy,
A My Horse, My Partner Book

from award-winning author
Lisa Wysocky

fura books

fura books

Published by
Fura Books
P.O. Box 90751
Nashville, TN 37209

The Library of Congress Cataloging-in-Publication Data Applied For
Lisa Wysocky—
Essential Horse Conformation: 51 Checkpoints Before You Buy,
A My Horse, My Partner Book
p. cm
ISBN-978-1-890224-01-1
1. Horses 2. Horse Conformation
I. Title
2018
Copyright 2018 by Lisa Wysocky

All Rights Reserved
including the right of reproduction in whole or in part in any form at any time.
Printed in the United States of America

3 5 7 9 10 8 6 4 2

For interviews, bulk purchases, or other information please contact
lisainfo@comcast.net, or LisaWysocky.com

The information in this book is meant to supplement, not replace, education and training about horses. Any activity involving horses poses some inherent risk. The author and publisher advise readers to take full responsibility for their safety and know their limits. Before practicing the ideas described in this book, be sure that any equipment you use is well maintained, and do not take risks beyond your level of experience, aptitude, training, and comfort level.

Dedication

To the many horses I have been
lucky enough to know and learn from.

Table of Contents

Introduction v
The Value of Conformation..1
The 51 Points 3

   1. Mouth 3
   2. Teeth 4
   3. Nostril 7
   4. Bridge of the Nose 8
   5. Forehead Whorl 9
   6. Eye...11
   7. Forehead 13
   8. Ear...13
   9. Poll 15
  10. Neck 16
  11. Chest 17
  12. Front Legs (overview) 19
  13. Knees 20
  14. Cannon Bones 21
  15. Amount of Bone 22
  16. Pastern and Fetlock 25
  17. Hoof 27
  18. Shoulder 31
  19. Profile 32

20. Withers 35
21. Posture... 37
22. Barrel.. 38
23. Stomach 40
24. Back 41
25. Loin.. 44
26. Croup 45
27. Rear Legs (overview) 45
28. Hip 46
29. Stifle 48
30. Hock 49
31. Rear Pastern and Fetlock 51
32. Tail 52
33. Muscle Tone 53
34. Scars and Blemishes 55
35. Skin and Hair 56
36. Weight.. 59
37. Size and Build 60
38. Range of Motion (overview) 62
39. Head and Neck Stretch 63
40. Nose to Chest Stretch 64
41. Front Leg Stretch... 65
42. Back Leg Stretch 67
43. Belly Lift 69
44. Tail Stretch 70
45. Gaits (overview)... 72
46. Backing 73
47. The Walk.. 74
48. The Trot 75
49. Gaited Horses 76
50. The Canter 77
51. Lameness 77

The Final Take-Away 81
After the Assessment 84
The Vet and Farrier Exam 86
Appendix A: Horse Assessment Form 88
Appendix B: The Ten-Minute Assessment 91
Appendix C: Parts of the Horse 94
Appendix D: Glossary 95
Acknowledgements 106

Additional Books by Lisa Wysocky

Nonfiction

The Power of Horses: True Stories from Country Music Stars

Success Within: How to Create the Greatest Moments of Your Life

Front of the Class: How Tourette Syndrome Made Me the Teacher I Never Had (with Brad Cohen)

My Horse, My Partner: Teamwork on the Ground (also available in DVD format)

Horse Country: A Celebration of Country Music and the Love of Horses

Two Foot Fred: How My Life Has Come Full Circle (with Fred Gill)

Success Talks: 101 Positive Things to Say to Yourself

Walking on Eggshells: Discovering Strength and Courage Amid Chaos (with Lyssa Chapman)

Horseback: A Memoir of My Early Years with Horses

Hidden Girl: The True Story of a Modern-Day Child Slave (with Shyima Hall)

Therapy Horse Selection: A My Horse, My Partner Book

Fiction

The Opium Equation: A Cat Enright Equestrian Mystery

The Magnum Equation: A Cat Enright Equestrian Mystery

The Fame Equation: A Cat Enright Equestrian Mystery

The Mane Equation: A Cat Enright Equestrian Mystery

Anthologies

Eight Mystery Writers You Should Be Reading Now

The Trouble with Cupid

Introduction

Most of you who have picked up this book already have a horse, or maybe you plan to purchase a horse sometime soon. Some of you might be new into this journey of horses, while others have been here for decades. My hope is that this book will be helpful to all.

As a trainer, instructor, clinician, and life-long student of the horse, I regularly hear stories from people whose horse ended up not being what they had hoped. Often, the disappointment revolves around the horse's physical inability to do the job intended. A barrel racing prospect has bucked shins, a cutting horse developed navicular, or an event horse came down with lower back problems. Suddenly the owner has an expensive pasture ornament, and a bitter taste in her mouth.

Just as a person who is six feet tall might not become the world's best jockey, the horse's conformation—or build—dictates what the horse is capable of. Want a smooth riding horse to trot out on the trail? Best not to choose a high withered horse with a high head carriage and a lot of knee action. Have a horse with a long back? As she ages, that horse might not be able to carry the weight that a short backed horse can. Knowing ahead of time what red flags you might find as you progress in your favorite horse activities, or as your horse ages, sets up realistic expectations and can head off disappointment.

I have had the extreme honor and privilege to be closely involved with many horses over many decades. In my experience, the most successful horses, the horses who flourish best with their owners and riders, are the ones who are there by careful selection, rather than by chance. These are the horses who passed pre-purchase vet exams with flying colors, and whose good conformation keeps them sound.

But how, exactly, do you find horses like that? And how do you know at first glance whether or not an individual horse has a good chance of becoming the best equine partner for you? These are the questions we will explore—along with answers, options, and ideas. My goal is to give you the tools; it is up to you to use them.

While personality, behavior, and training are also very important considerations when choosing a horse, we will concentrate here solely on conformation, for if the horse cannot physically do what you expect, the rest all become moot points.

Please consider this a helpful guide for horse lovers of all disciplines and all levels of experience, rather than an all-encompassing tomb on conformation. Instead of a detailed lesson on anatomy, the basic conformation points covered here relate to an assessment you can do of your existing horse(s), or of a potential new horse. Think of it as a road map to avoid pitfalls, and to understand the many red flags you might encounter in choosing a horse, or in making activity decisions about an existing horse in your herd.

If your potential new equine is a mule, or a hinny or a jenny, you will also find some of the information here useful. While the body is different on all equines, most of the information regarding leg structure and tracking, condition, skin and hair, flexion and other areas will still be applicable.

There also are many more parts of the horse to look at when discussing conformation than are covered here, and many of them are points that can be discussed in deeper depth elsewhere. But, the fifty-one points mentioned here are designed to help you either weed out, or confirm, the vast majority of your horse choices.

Happy reading,

Lisa Wysocky

Lisa Wysocky
November 2018

The Value of Conformation

Conformation is the build of the horse, but there are so many related subjects that tie closely into it that you cannot mention one without the others—soundness and functionality included.

Whenever I first look at a horse, I do a nose to tail conformation assessment. When you first begin to do these, it may take an hour or more to look at each part of the horse, assess it, and then put the parts together to create a whole. Only then can you make an informed decision as to whether this particular horse is perfect for your needs. After you have done several dozen of these assessments, it may only take you ten or fifteen minutes to go nose to tail. And, if you have a specific purpose in mind for the horse, then you may be able to tell in less than a minute whether or not this is the horse for you.

After you have evaluated a number of horses, you will also start to see some patterns taking place. While there are many exceptions to the rule, you will begin to see that a horse with a higher neck carriage often has an up and down movement to his stride, rather than the longer, flatter movement of a horse with a lower neck carriage. You will find that a horse with a straight shoulder has a choppier trot, while a horse who has a big, sloping shoulder can more easily extend a gait.

It's true that conformation is more important for a horse who will be ridden, driven, or vaulted on, than a horse who will solely do ground work. Over time, however, all poorly conformed horses have a greater chance of developing a lameness, and or stiffness or arthritis, than do horses with better conformation. This can mean high medical costs—or extra costs for supplements—no matter the level of activity.

Carrying the thought on, a lame or stiff horse often develops bad behavior, because he or she is uncomfortable. So, no matter what the intended job for the horse is, it is good to understand how well the horse might be able to do that job in five or ten years. A good evaluation of the horse's conformation is one element that will help with that understanding.

This kind of assessment is also a good, annual tool to evaluate your own horses as they age. By learning to look at each of the fifty-one points mentioned, you can spot the wobbly hock that recently developed on your gelding, or notice that your twenty-year-old mare's back has started to sway. Having this information is important, so you can make decisions on your horse's activity level based on his or her best interest.

While many generalizations will be made in the following pages, think of them as something to consider, just as a doctor might consider that a child with a rash could have poison ivy. Or, the child could have a food allergy. Nothing is set in stone, and all of the details are parts of the whole. The final choice, of course, is yours.

The Fifty-One Points

As you find a horse and go through the assessment, be sure to take detailed notes. Photos and videos can be helpful, too. There is an assessment form on page 88 that may be useful. Or, go to LisaWysocky.com to find a downloadable pdf file of the form.

If you are not an experienced horse person, when looking at a horse it is always a good idea to find someone who is to go along with you. Even if you are full of knowledge about horses, a second brain and pair of eyes is always helpful. The knowledge and experience of this second person may just save you from a lot of expense and heartbreak.

It is easy to fall in love with every horse you see, and not so easy to pass on a horse you love, but who may be unsuitable for you. Your friend can help you leave those unsuitable horses with their current owners. Okay, let's get started!

1. Mouth

I call this a nose to tail assessment, but we really start with the mouth, and the mouth of the horse you look at should be relaxed. You can see a tense mouth in the tightness of the corners of the lips, and in the lower lip. A tense mouth can indicate the horse's state of mind. Some deductive reasoning may tell you why the horse is tense, but even if you never know why, it is enough to know that he or she is.

From the side, you will also want to see if the horse is shallow mouthed, or if the mouth is of normal length. This is personal preference, but many trainers prefer a horse with a shallow mouth, as they feel these horses are more responsive to the bit. Others feel differently, but there is enough of a debate that it has to be mentioned here.

2. Teeth

A horse's teeth can tell you many things. The first indication to look for is whether or not the horse is a cribber. Cribbing is a compulsive behavior where the horse grabs a solid object with her teeth, such as a stall door or fence rail, then pulls against the object and sucks in air. Over time, cribbing can wear the front teeth down to nubs—and also destroy your nice, wood fences. Plus, cribbing has been linked as a cause of colic and stomach ulcers. Horses usually start to crib out of boredom, but once the habit starts, it is very difficult to break. You can tell if the horse is a confirmed cribber if his top front teeth are very short.

If you are unsure, and if the opportunity arises, at some point during the assessment casually stand the horse in front of a wood fence or panel. Keep the horse on a loose lead as you talk to the horse's owner. If, after five minutes the horse has made no move to grab the wood and suck in air, then the horse has a good chance of being okay in this area.

Windsucking is a related vice where the horse arches her neck and inhales air, without grabbing on to anything. Boredom is the root of this behavior, too, so the five-minute downtime may also root out a windsucker.

In addition to the possibilities of cribbing and windsucking, teeth can tell you the age of the horse. The sad truth is that some horse owners pass off horses as being younger than they are. Just as in our own pop culture, in the horse world, youth often rocks.

Veterinarians and seasoned horse people can often estimate the age of a horse with just a glance at his teeth. For others it is a very difficult task, especially when the horse isn't keen on showing his pearly whites. Here are two relatively easy ways to get a broad estimate of the age of a horse.

The first is a side view of the horse's front teeth. To see the teeth, part the horse's lips on the side of his mouth. Then look for the angle of the front teeth as you view them from the side. If the top and bottom teeth meet in a mostly vertical plane, then the

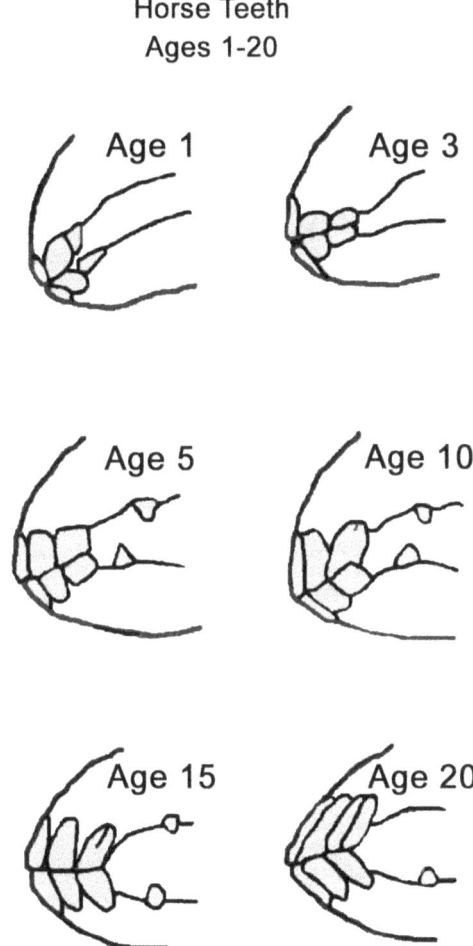

horse is young. The greater the angle where the top and bottom teeth meet: the older the horse.

GALVAYNE'S GROOVE

Age 10
Age 15
Age 20
Age 25
Age 30

The second way to tell how old a horse is, especially an older horse, is to look for Galvayne's Groove. Professor Sydney Galvayne (1846-1913) was born in the United Kingdom. A lifelong student of the horse, some considered him a horse trainer of sorts, but others saw him as a skilled self-promoter. In either case, while Galvayne did not discover the method of telling how old a horse was by looking at a groove in the teeth, he was the first to popularize it. More than a hundred years later, this interesting tooth groove still carries his name.

This groove occurs on the #3 upper corner incisors, and produces a vertical line beginning when the horse is ten years old. It reaches halfway down the tooth by age fifteen, and is completely down the tooth at age twenty. The groove then begins to disappear from the top of the tooth and is half gone by age twenty-five, and undetectable by age thirty. It is a simple thing to lift up the side of the horse's upper lip to see if the groove is there, and where it lies on the tooth.

The last area to check when it comes to the teeth is if the upper or lower teeth actually meet, or if the horse has an overbite or an underbite. A severe shortening of the lower jaw is called parrot mouth, and many breed associations do not allow registry of parrot-mouthed horses. This is because when the top and bottom teeth do not meet, it is hard for the horse to eat properly. It doesn't seem to be as much of a problem if the lower teeth stick out farther than the upper, maybe because the condition is most often not nearly as severe.

3. Nostril

Just as with humans, the nostril brings air into the lungs, and a large nostril means more air can get in. If you will ride your horse on long trail rides, or if you live in higher elevations or in a very

This horse's large nostrils help keep her cool during hot summers in Tennessee.

hot or cold climate, a big nostril could be important, as a horse with a big nostril will have more endurance for exercise and weather extremes. Larger nostrils also help heavy horses, such as drafts and draft crosses, bring in enough air.

The nostril is also used to pull scent in, so the horse can determine safety. The bigger the nostril, the more scent that can be categorized. Scent is also important in the horse's social structure within the herd. You may have noticed that most horses greet humans as they do other horses, with their nose. Upon meeting a new horse, allowing him or her to smell the back of your hand quickly shows the horse that you are friend, rather than foe. Some people will breathe into a horse's nose, and that accomplishes pretty much the same thing.

4. Bridge of the Nose

This Thoroughbred gelding's nose shows a nice, refined dish.

Another conformation trait to look for is the curve of the bridge of the nose. Look at the horse from the side. Does the nose dish in, or curve out? Some of what you see is breed specific. The Arabian is just one breed that dishes in, while draft horses often bulge out. The outward curve is called a Roman nose, and oddly enough, many trainers feel that a good number of horses with Roman noses can be stubborn. Not all, by any means, but some may make you work very hard for results.

At the least, a Roman nose is not thought to be a positive trait with many light breed associations. With a draft such as a Shire or Clydesdale, however, it is more accepted.

5. Forehead Whorl

Centuries ago, horsemen in Arabia thought the whorl pattern (or cowlick) in the center of a horse's forehead indicated how easy the horse might be to train. Gypsies in Europe, who are well known for their bond with horses, thought so, too—as do many horsemen and horsewomen today.

Generally, most people who have made a study of this interesting phenomenon agree that the most willing horses are those with one whorl centered on the forehead directly between the eyes. Others feel a whorl centered below the eyes is also positive.

On the other hand, the theory goes, if a horse has two (or more) swirls spread out on the face it could mean that the horse has a difficult personality. I personally have worked with two such horses and while they were definitely a challenge, in the end they both made terrific therapy horses.

Years ago popular author and horsewoman Linda Tellington-Jones analyzed answers on a survey that was sent to horse owners. The completed surveys contained information on whorl patterns and behavior of fifteen hundred different horses and, for the most part, confirmed the following data:

- One whorl in the center of the forehead meant the horse was willing.

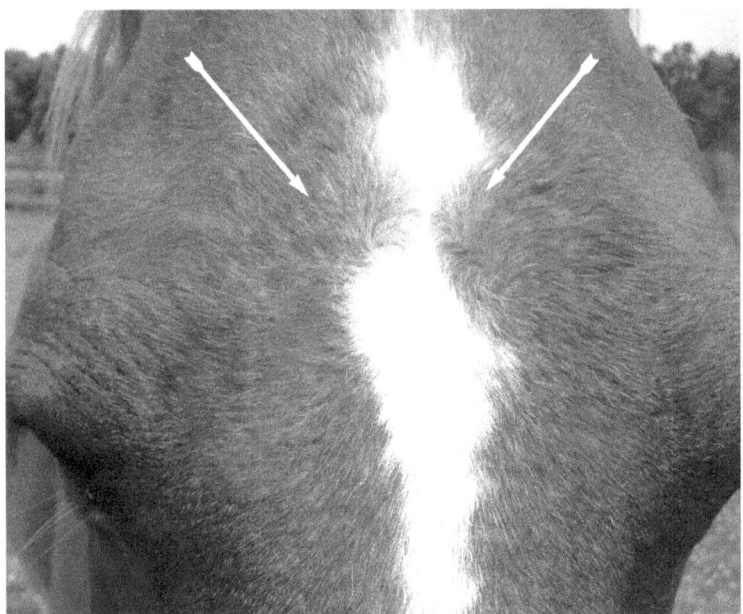

This double whorled mare is both a herd leader and a challenge. But she is also steady, and an excellent teacher.

- One whorl below the eyes indicated intelligence.
- One long whorl between or running below the eyes indicated a friendly, agreeable horse.
- Two or more whorls on the forehead indicated a complicated personality.

If you are fascinated by the idea that a whorl can determine personality, pick up a copy of *Getting in TTouch: Understand and Influence Your Horse's Personality* by Linda Tellington-Jones.

In addition to Tellington-Jones, English, Irish, and Polish studies all found that about 75 percent of the time left-footed horses have counter-clockwise hair whorls, and horses that favor their right side have clockwise whorls. These studies also determined that horses with a single whorl above their eyes were more difficult, and that horses with a single whorl below or between their eyes were easier to handle. Horses with long whorls or double whorls also acted the most cautiously when coming up to an unfamiliar object.

In addition to whorls on the forehead, like dogs and cattle, horses can have whorls on other areas of their body, such as their chest, stomach, and neck—as well as other areas. Several universities are now studying these whorls to see if there is additional correlation to personality.

The reason whorl patterns and personality are believed to be connected is, because before a foal is born, whorl patterns and the part of the brain that determines personality form at the same time. So, should you turn down a double whorled horse? Probably not. As with everything else discussed here, it is one piece of the whole. In addition, the horse's life experiences and training can modify what nature may or may not have given him in the way of whorl patterns and behavior. Whorls are, simply, something to consider.

6. Eye

Moving to the eye, look for eyes that are widely-spaced. A horse whose eyes are toward the side of her head, versus toward the front, can see around her more easily. A typical horse can see almost 360 degrees around her body. There is a triangular blind spot directly in front of and behind the horse that extends about four feet out from the horse's body, but a horse with a narrow face, versus a triangular one, will have a more limited range of sight.

A horse who can't see well might spook. In addition, because a horse can't see as far around himself as other horses can, he could be nervous. Remember that, to a horse, *everything* is about being safe. If a horse can't see that he is safe, then he will be more on edge than a horse who can. Of course, horses use other senses to determine safety. Sight is just one of the tools a horse incorporates. But, a smaller range of vision limits a horse's ability to determine safety. Also look for a soft, kind eye. You'll know it when you see it. An eye that is dull can mean the horse is depressed, or the horse might be sick or in pain.

This Appaloosa has a triangular face with eyes set wide on the side of his head. A white sclera can be seen at the front of his otherwise soft eye.

In general, an eye that looks startled could mean the horse is jumpy. With the exception of the Appaloosa, the Pony of the Americas (POA), and several other less common breeds, if you can see a white rim, or sclera, around the eye, much like the white of a human eye, the horse might be a bit too "up." The Appaloosa, POA, and a few other breeds have been bred for many decades to show a white sclera. It is also sometimes seen in Paint horses, but if you see a lot of white around the eye in other breeds, it might be a minor red flag for you to consider.

Blindness is also a consideration and sometimes it is hard to tell how good a horse's vision actually is. You can wave your hand two or three feet in front of the horse's eye to see if the horse responds with a head toss or a blink, but a placid, comfortable horse many not react, even if she sees very clearly. A veterinarian can always check the horse's quality of vision during the vet check, if you get that far with this horse.

Some horses will have an eye that is misshapen by an injury, or he or she may have been born with a misshapen eye. As a rule, horses who do not have good vision do not do well going into new situations, although horses who start with good vision and gradually lose it often adapt well if they are able to stay in familiar surroundings. FYI: a study in Liverpool, England found that 87 percent of horses age fifteen or older had cataracts or some other vision issue. There are exceptions to every rule, though, so keep an open mind until your entire assessment is complete.

7. Forehead

Moving up, is the horse's forehead bulging or flat? Can you feel the bones underneath the horse's forelock, or is there a lot of padding there? Some breeds, such as the Arabian, have more padding here, but most horses do not. If a Thoroughbred or Quarter Horse, for example, has a large bulge here, it could be an indication of chewing difficulties and/or tooth problems, and you might consider having an equine dentist take a look.

Be sure to look at both sides of the forehead, as it is possible that there is a bulge on one side and not the other, which again, could be a tooth or chewing issue on just the left or right side.

8. Ear

Most horse lovers know that the ear is the window to the horse's brain, so whatever your prospective horse's ear is pointed at, that is what she is thinking about. The positioning of the ear is not as important as the movement of the ear. However, a few trainers feel that a horse who has ears set low, toward the sides of her head, can be slower to respond to a stimulus or a cue. This is not always a bad thing, and depends on what you expect the horse to do. Ear size is often dependant on the breed. Arabians and stock horses such as the Quarter Horse, Appaloosa, and Paint can have small, dainty ears, whereas a Thoroughbred or Clydesdale may have ears that look gigantic.

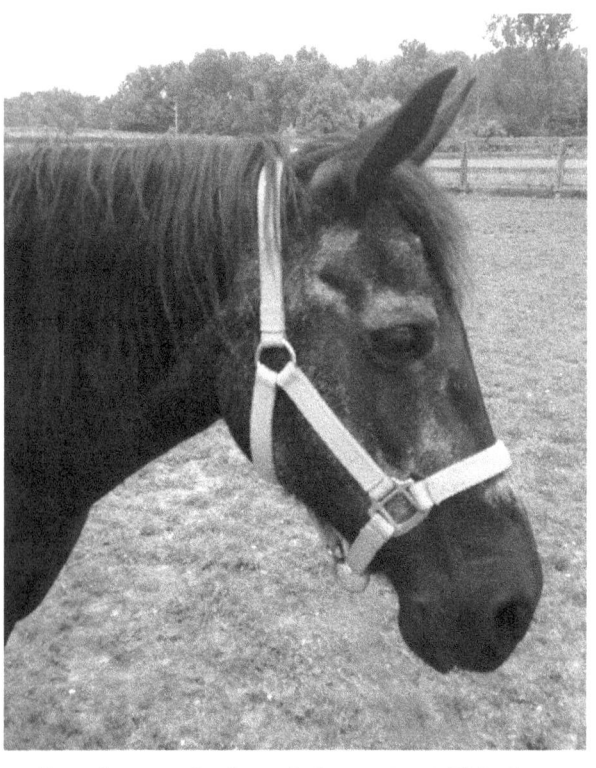

Ear size can be breed dependent. This large pony is a Tennessee Walking horse cross. Her big ears and advanced age give her face character.

Size aside, the ear should swivel when there is sound to the horse's side or behind. A good way to test this is when the horse is relaxed, which may not be at the beginning of your evaluation.

But, at the right moment, stand twenty feet off the horse's hip and clap your hands or make an odd noise. The horse's ear should swivel toward the sound, and she may even turn her head to look for the source of the sound. You may want to repeat the exercise to the other side, also standing far back behind the horse. I never like to stand directly behind the horse's tail, but you can try fifteen or twenty feet behind the left or right hock, where the horse still has some visual of you, and where you are well beyond kicking distance.

If the horse has no response to the noises, there is a chance that the horse is hard of hearing, or even deaf. This possibility increases if the horse is older. If the horse also has a dull eye, the horse may have heard the sound but has shut down emotionally. Illness is another possibility. Another option is that the horse is so secure in her environment that she already trusts you to keep her safe. Some sort of a response is a good thing, because you do want the horse engaged, so try again in a few minutes.

9. Poll

Next, touch the horse's poll, the small bump behind the horse's ears. If the horse pulls away, consider that the horse might feel tightness or discomfort there. Sometimes, horse who are ridden with a lot of collection can become sore in the poll area. Dental problems, continual yanking on the halter, even stretching a neck to reach under a fence to graze can cause problems in the poll.

While not a conformation issue *per se*, if the horse's poll is sore, it will affect just about every other part of her body. The soreness, if continued over a period of time, could make her walk unevenly or develop muscles differently on the left and right sides of her body. Back soreness and poor behavior could also develop.

Often, horses who are considered "ear shy," or hard to bridle, are simply sore in the poll. If you have a concern here, an equine massage therapist, chiropractor, veterinarian, or energy worker may be able to give more info.

10. Neck

Because the horse bobs his neck up and down to propel himself forward, the size, shape, and positioning of the neck is critical to your intended activity for the horse. Depending on the horse's breed, the neck of the horse you look at may be long or short, fat or thin. The important thing is that the size and shape of the neck fits the rest of the horse.

If you are looking at a gelding who is supposed to be a registered Thoroughbred, and he has a short, cresty neck, it might make you think he is not fully Thoroughbred. At the very least, this horse is probably not the best hunter prospect. A short, thick neck and throatlatch is often found on round, heavy horses, and these horses can be prone to founder or Cushings syndrome.

Cushings occurs in horses when a tumor develops in the pituitary gland. As the tumor slowly grows, it sends inappropriate signals to the rest of the body to produce lots of hormones, especially the stress hormone cortisol. Too much cortisol can be a factor in laminitis (founder), mouth ulcers, large fat deposits along the neck, excessive thirst and urination, and very long hair. Collectively, this is referred to as Cushings.

Laminitis is an inflammation within the hoof that can cause the third phalanx, a bone in the hoof that is also called the coffin bone, to rotate and cause permanent lameness. Some horses founder so badly that they cannot be saved. If the horse you are evaluating has a fat neck (or a fat, lumpy neck), Cushings and laminitis are things to consider in the long-term management of the horse. In your pre-purchase vet exam, you may also want the horse's feet to be x-rayed to be sure founder has not already occurred.

Generally speaking, a horse with a long neck is more athletic than a horse who has one that is short, as there is more length that the horse can use to balance himself. Also, a horse with a neck that rises upward, versus one that stretches out horizontally in front of him, will give the horse more up and down movement, especially at the trot. The horse will also have more elevation off the ground, and more knee and hock action. You may have ridden a horse whose springy trot made it difficult not to post too high. That horse probably had a neck that rose upward. Think Saddlebred.

This big movement at the trot can actually be beneficial as it teaches riders to get—and keep—their heels down. If the heels come up, the big movement will throw the rider forward. It doesn't take too many times of that happening before a rider's heels stay consistently down.

You may want a horse who provides a smoother ride. If so, look for a horse with a horizontal neckline such as the stock type breeds usually provide. The trots are smoother, and usually there is less movement at the walk.

A gaited horse, depending on the breed, will have a neck of good length with some elevation, and usually will provide smooth movement at the walk and gait.

11. Chest

Next, view the width of the horse's chest from the front. Depending on your needs you may be looking for a wide-chested horse

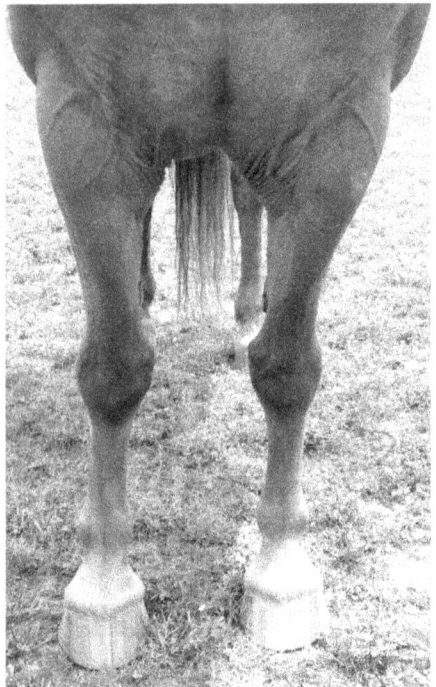 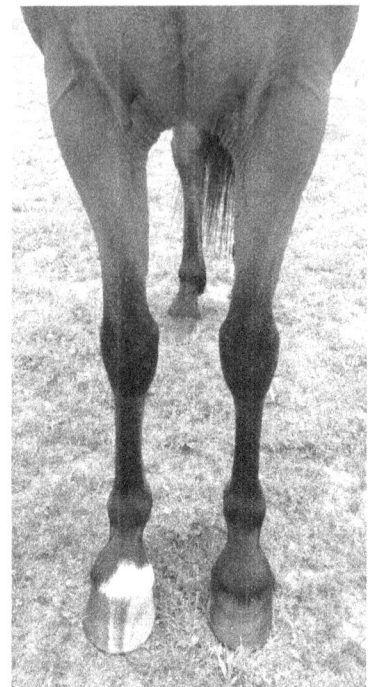

Both of these horses are 15.2, but you can easily see the very different widths of their chests and the length of their legs.

or a narrow one. Narrow chested horses are often found in gaited breeds, such as the Tennessee Walking Horse or Spotted Saddle Horse, and in the Arabian and some Thoroughbreds.

Wider chested horses can be found in the Haflinger, Fjord, draft crosses, and stock horse breeds (Quarter Horse, Appaloosa, and Paint). Many ponies also are wider, although the Hackney pony and some other pony breeds can be very narrow.

The advantage with a wide chest is that it usually also provides a broad back, and many riders balance better with a wider base. Keep in mind, though, that there are variations in every horse. Just because a horse is an Arabian, don't assume that the chest will be narrow. That's another reason a thorough assessment of each individual horse is so important.

Also, when the horse is standing squarely, look for equal muscling on the left and right sides of the chest. If one side is more muscled than the other, there could be muscle atrophy from an injury, or it could be that the sport the horse does, such as playing polo, has developed the musculature differently on each side.

12. Front Legs (overview)

The front end of the horse carries roughly two thirds of the horse's weight, so it is critical that your horse's front legs be functional and sound. Finding a horse with perfect legs is impossible, but if one front leg turns east and the other west, it is likely that your horse is bound for eventual soreness and possible lameness. Besides the fact that a horse with less than desirable front legs might be hurting (no one likes to see that), hurting and soreness can cause behavior problems.

To look at the front legs, have the horse stand squarely, with all four legs evenly underneath her. Then from the front of the horse, imagine a vertical line dropping from the center of the top of the horse's front leg, all the way down to the ground. Does the vertical line follow the top of the leg, through the center of the knee, and down the center of the cannon bone? Does it drop down the center of the horse's hoof?

If this horse stands with her feet close together, meaning the straight line you dropped from the top of the leg falls to the outside of the hoof, she is "base narrow." This can cause a horse to bear weight unevenly, and could lead to arthritis. Reverse the issue, standing with feet too far apart, so the vertical line falls to the inside of the hoof, places stress on the inner legs and can also cause

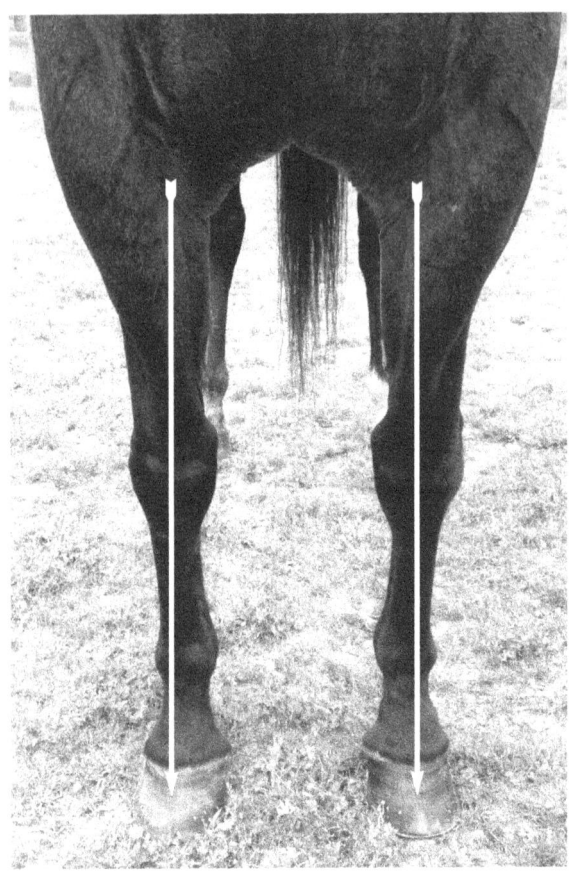

This horse is relatively straight in his upper leg, but has cannon bones and fetlocks that narrow in, and toes that point slightly out.

arthritis, especially in the pastern and coffin bone.

Most horses do not have faultless front leg conformation. As long as the degree to which the legs are off is not severe, there probably is no cause for worry.

But, if the legs have knees that point inward or outward, cannon bones that extend downward from the left or right of the knee, rather than the center, or if the horse is greatly knock-kneed or bowlegged, it could be a red flag.

13. Knees

When it comes to the knees, they should be flat, even in size, and not angled inward or outward. Puffy knees can indicate an injury such as bone chips, which may be quite painful. And, knees that are uneven in size are a cause for concern, as one knee might be weaker than the other. I have even seen a few horses who have one knee set higher on one leg than the other.

Knock knees that angle toward each other, or bow-knees that bow away can be weaker than knees that face straight ahead. The lower part of the leg usually follows the knee, so if the knee points outward, then the lower leg and hoof probably will, too. Each horse is different, though, so look closely.

Next, from the side, see if the horse is "over" at the knee; or under, back at (or "calf") kneed. Being over at the knee is the lesser conformational sin, with some trainers preferring jumpers and other active horses to be a bit over. A calf-kneed horse might develop any number of knee troubles over time, however, especially if you ask her to go long distances or compete in a challenging sport.

You may know a person who has "bad knees" and know how this condition can limit his or her activity. Horses are no different. If a joint is weak, or if it hurts, they will not be able to go long distances, or perform well.

14. Cannon Bones

Cannon bones are the long bones below the knee and hock. They should be smooth, and free of bumps and blemishes. Some horses have splints, which is a hard, bony swelling on the inside of the front leg, just below the knee. The splint lies either between the splint bone and cannon bone or on the splint bone itself. They can be caused by poor conformation, hard work, or trauma, and usually are painful when first formed. After a few months, though, the splint "cools" and does not usually cause problems.

One caveat, however. If you plan to show your horse in any kind of conformation class, a splint can be considered a blemish. While not a huge fault, in otherwise equal horses, a splint can be the difference between first and second place.

Another issue can be bone or calcium deposits along the cannon bone. We have a horse at Colby's Army, a therapeutic riding center where I am the executive director. Quincy, whom you can see on the cover of the book, had a severe injury to his right front pastern when he was young. The injury was so severe that a decade later, when x-rayed, the barbed wire scars could still be seen on the bone. That said, Quincy had great careers as a low level eventer, third-level Dressage horse, and trail horse.

When Quincy was about fifteen, though, the years of use caught up with him, and he began to put calcium deposits down the inside of his right cannon bone. It probably was his body's way of ensuring strength in the injured leg. The calcium deposits presented as three large bumps below where a splint would be, and he was quite sore for a time. Over the course of six months, the bumps filled in and the soreness went away. On x-ray, the deposits are seen as an added area to the bone. Today, at nineteen, he is serviceably sound and enjoys his lightweight riders.

Lastly, look for scars on the skin around the cannon bone. Because there is little to no fat here, a scar can more easily interfere with functionality than a scar on the horse's neck or rump. Also, a pattern of white, scar-like dots can mean the horse was pin-fired in an attempt to heal a sore tendon.

15. Amount of Bone

The amount of bone in the cannon bone is good to note. The term "bone" indicates the thickness or heaviness of the leg. An Arabian or Paso Fino will have less bone than a draft or draft cross. The amount of bone comes into play if there is not enough of it to support the rest of the horse. Years ago some stock horse breeders bred slim, delicate legs onto some big bodied horses. The result? Much lameness and an increase in navicular disease. Navicular entails inflammation of the navicular bone and surrounding tissue in the front feet and can lead to extreme, degenerative lameness that is difficult, if not impossible, to cure. Sound horses that do not have a lot of bone typically have narrow chests and are slimmer in build.

The amount of bone is a big factor in the amount of weight a horse can carry. If this is a concern, know that the maximum weight a horse can carry varies by breed, age, size, conditioning, conformation, and the level of work she will be expected to do. Generally speaking, a light-framed, 15-hand horse can carry less weight than a stoutly built horse of the same age and size.

Measuring a horse's cannon bone is one way to figure out how much weight can be placed on a horse's back, but there are also two other methods you can use.

Method #1: Measuring the Cannon Bone

1. With an accurate cloth tape measure, measure the circumference of the front cannon bone, just below the knee. Keep that number handy. Don't have a cloth measure? Use a piece of baling twine, wrap it snugly, but not tightly, around the cannon bone, mark the place where the end of the twine meets the beginning, and place the length along a ruler to get the measurement.

2. Add (A) the true weight of the horse + (B) the weight of the rider + (C) the weight of the tack.

3. Divide the total of #2 by #1 (the cannon bone circumference measurement).

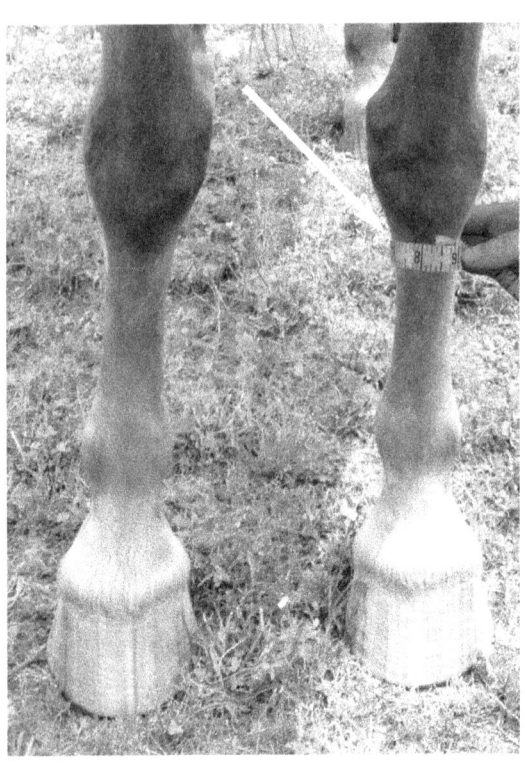

4. Divide the result of #3 by two.

You might have come out with a number that is between 75 and 85. If the number is higher than 85, the horse is probably not big or stout enough for your needs. Or, try lightening up the weight of your tack.

Method #2:
20 Percent Rule

In this method, a thousand-pound horse can carry 20 percent of his weight, or two hundred pounds of rider and tack. The key is in knowing exactly how much the horse weighs, which can be difficult if you do not have a scale for the horse to stand on. Most of the commercial weight tapes are inaccurate, but sometimes a local county agricultural extension agent will come out to weigh a horse. Or, if you have a trailer to transport the horse, and the current owner is willing, you can ask a local feed mill if they have a scale you can walk the horse onto.

In using this method, if the horse is seriously overweight, use his ideal weight, rather than what he weighs right now. Know that many people use a 20 percent formula for younger horses, and a 16 percent formula for older horses, because as horses age, it becomes harder for them to carry weight. Finally, many feel that stout ponies can carry more than 20 percent of their weight, so a 25 percent formula for a healthy pony in good condition would not be out of line.

Method #3: Divide by Six
This formula works well to determine an appropriate weight for an older horse, or a horse who is coming out of rehab or layoff. Just divide the horse's actual weight by six to give the total weight (including rider and tack) that the horse can carry. For example, a thousand-pound horse can carry up to 166 pounds.

While you probably can't accurately determine the horse's weight when you first look at him, an experienced horse person can ballpark it, as long as you take a cloth tape measure with you. In this manner, you can determine if the horse is big (or small) enough for your needs.

16. Pastern and Fetlock

Moving down the leg from the side, the angle of the pastern should match the angle of the shoulder. The pastern and the joint nearest it, the fetlock, are both shock absorbers. That's why the length of the pastern is also important. Long pasterns provide a springy ride, and short ones a choppier gait. Pasterns that are too long can be weak, and the horse can develop trouble with suspensory ligaments and flexor tendons that can affect the fetlock joint. A pastern that is too long also reduces the amount of speed the horse has, because it takes longer to push off, and to get the foot off the ground. Longer pasterns are usually seen on Thoroughbreds, Saddlebreds, and many breeds of gaited horses.

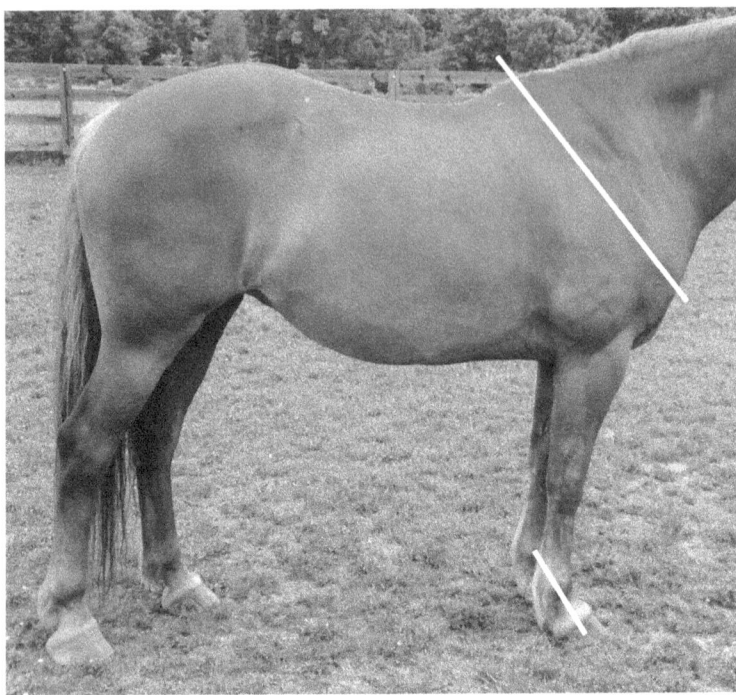

The very short, upright pasterns, along with the straight shoulder ensures this Belgian/Quarter Horse mare has a ground-pounding trot.

You see shorter pasterns on draft horses, draft crosses, and some stock horses—horses who also have lots of strength, short legs, and straight shoulders. A too-short pastern is almost always too upright, and creates a pile-driving pounding effect, especially at the trot. In addition, look for short pasterns on horses who are base-narrow and who toe in. In horses who are built like this, over time you might expect arthritis to flare up in the fetlock, cannon bone, pastern, or hoof. The horse could also develop navicular from the extra demands on the bones and joints in the pastern and hoof.

Two other areas to look for in the pastern are ringbone and sidebone. Ringbone is an arthritic-based condition that involves deterioration of cartilage and formation of additional bone in the pastern and coffin joints. It can be caused by injury, strain from athletic activity, or poor conformation. Horses with straight pasterns and upright legs have a higher risk for ringbone because there is more force placed on the pastern and coffin joints.

While an x-ray will make sure, you can feel for ringbone possibilities around the coronet band. Look for swelling there, or around the pastern, especially on the front and sides of the leg. Some horses are not much bothered by ringbone, while others seem to be in chronic pain. If you suspect a horse has ringbone, it likely will affect her endurance and athletic ability over time.

Sidebone is similar to ringbone, but mostly affects the coffin bone, and is only seen on the sides of the coronet band or pastern. It is often seen in heavy, older horses when their ligaments lose elasticity.

17. Hoof

Unfortunately, not everyone takes care of their horse's hooves properly, especially when they want to find the horse another home. Hopefully, the horse you are assessing has had a recent trim or shoe reset, but do not be surprised if she hasn't.

Long, untrimmed feet can make the horse stand awkwardly and it can be hard to get an accurate assessment of the horse's conformation if this is the case. Long toes can throw off shoulder and pastern angles, posture, and gait. Sometimes you have to use a "best guess," or even your imagination.

Specifics to look for within the hoof include vertical cracks, as these can be difficult, lengthy, and expensive to make go away. Severe cracks will also make it difficult for a horse to perform at his best.

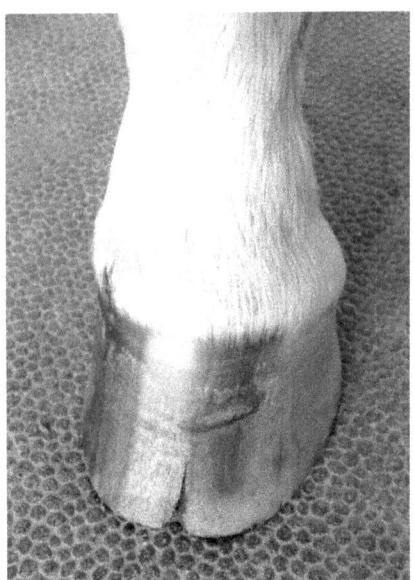

A vertical split may or may not cause lameness. A crack such as this may also cause the horse to compensate on other limbs and become sore across his hips, shoulders, and back.

The hardness and thickness of the hoof wall is also important. Some horses are prone to "shelly" or crumbly hooves. These hooves break down easily if the horse is barefoot, or if the hoof wall is too thin to hold a shoe nail. Nutrition and environmental factors, such as an extremely dry climate, play a part in the shelly hoof, but so do genetics, injury, and lack of trimming.

Some draft or heavy horses are prone to a flare of the hoof, especially near the heel. A flare is actually a separation of the hoof wall from the coffin bone. Flares can be caused by many things and can happen to any horse. Usually the condition can be corrected, and often it is not serious, but if left untreated, it can become painful. Genetics, founder, lack of trimming, and an extremely wet climate can all contribute, but as with shelly hooves, you may have to use your detecting skills to find out both the cause and the solution.

The horse could also have a club foot (where the toe is short, heel is tall, and the pastern angle is very steep), or a coon foot (where the toe is long, heel is short, and the pastern angle is very low.) There is such a thing as "high-low syndrome," and it occurs with horses who have tall legs and short necks. To graze, or to eat hay from the ground, these horses have to place one foot ahead of the other to get their head low enough to eat. Over time, the leg that is put forward grows a long toe and short heel, and the leg placed underneath for support wears off at the toe and grows a long heel. You can't shorten legs or grow a longer neck, but you can feed this kind of horse hay from a raised feeder and have shoes put on to even out the growth.

Note that front hooves will be rounder in shape, while rear hooves will be more oblong. This is because the horse balances most of his weight on his front end.

After looking closely at the outer part of the hooves, pick one up. The hoof sole could be flat, instead of cup shaped, making the horse more prone to stone bruises. You could also discover contracted heels, white line disease, or thrush. While none of these are earth shattering, they can be time consuming to cure. While you'd like

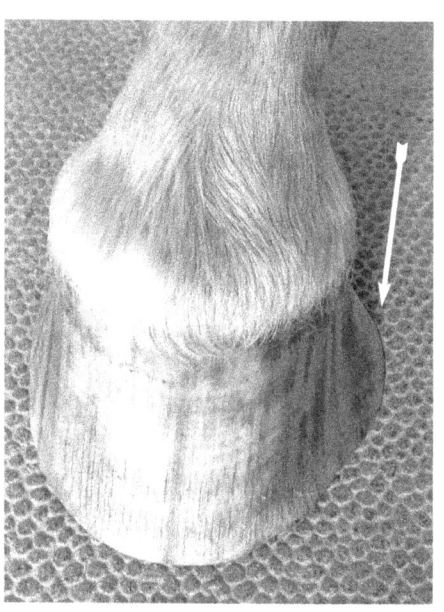

This kind of flare is often seen on draft horses and on draft crosses.

each hoof to look healthy, each can look very different, so it is best to look at the underside of each hoof, rather than just one.

The underside of the hoof should show even wear on each side of the hoof wall. If the horse is shod, you can check the wear patterns on the shoe, rather than the hoof wall. If you see uneven wear, either on the shoe or the hoof wall, the horse puts more weight on one side of the hoof than the other. It may be because the horse toes in or out, or that the horse is sore.

In addition to the shape of the hoof, where it points is of interest. Straight ahead is ideal, but that is not always the case. Toeing in, or pointing the toes toward each other, causes the horse to place more weight on the outside of their feet. This puts stress on the inner part of the leg, all the way from hoof to the shoulder. If the horse toes out (she may also stand base wide) she will bear more weight on the inside of the foot. This can cause shoeing or trimming difficulties, and over time, cause soreness and arthritis.

This Walking horse's dark leg shows a striped hoof.

Some horses, however, do quite well no matter which way their feet point.

A brief note on hoof color, which can range from light tan to black, to every shade between. Some horses even have vertical stripes on their hooves. As a rule, a horse with a white stocking that goes down to the hoof wall will have a light hoof. A horse with a dark lower leg will have a dark hoof. The exception is a white horse who may technically be gray. Many gray horses are born black and then "gray" out. These horses have dark skin and hooves, unless he or she has a white stocking.

Some people feel that light hooves are softer than dark. An old cowboy saying is: *Four white feet and a white nose, cut off his head and throw him to the crows.* Of course, we don't want to do that! But back in the 1800s, on ranches when there was little in the way of hoof care (or sunburn care for noses), one can see that a horse with dark hooves and a dark nose might be preferable for the cowboy who was out on the range for weeks at a time. Many farriers, however, will tell you that a light hoof is just as good as a darker one.

A few breeds, such as the Appaloosa and Pony of the Americas, have vertical stripes on the hoof wall. Because Appaloosas, Quarter Horses, and Paint horses have some of the same foundation sires, you can sometimes see striped hooves in the latter two breeds, and even with select horses in just about any breed.

The bottom line is whether or not the hoof is healthy enough for the horse's intended purpose. Will the hoof hold up for the activities the horse will be doing? And, how much will it cost to maintain the hoof? You might not have the funds needed to care for a horse who will incur higher than average veterinarian or farrier bills.

18. Shoulder

Moving your eye up to the horse's shoulder, it is best to look at it from the side. Be sure to stand far enough away to get an overall look. Many who study conformation teach that the ideal shoulder is at a 45-degree angle, but across so many breeds and breed types, my experience is that the soundest horses have a shoulder angle that matches the angle of the pastern.

A straighter shoulder angle gives the horse a more up and down movement of the leg, a shorter stride, and a choppier trot. A shoulder with a greater angle will give a long, flat stride and smoother trot. This is another reason to have a clear vision of your needs for the horse before you look. There are exceptions to this rule, though. At Colby's Army we have a Thoroughbred/draft cross with a very straight shoulder; short, straight pasterns; and a nice, smooth trot.

19. Profile

Next, stand about fifteen feet away when the horse is quiet and standing with his feet squarely underneath him, and while he is weight-bearing on all four feet.

Your first look at the horse's profile should note the height of the horse's withers as compared to the horse's hip (or the high point where the loin merges into the croup). Which is higher?

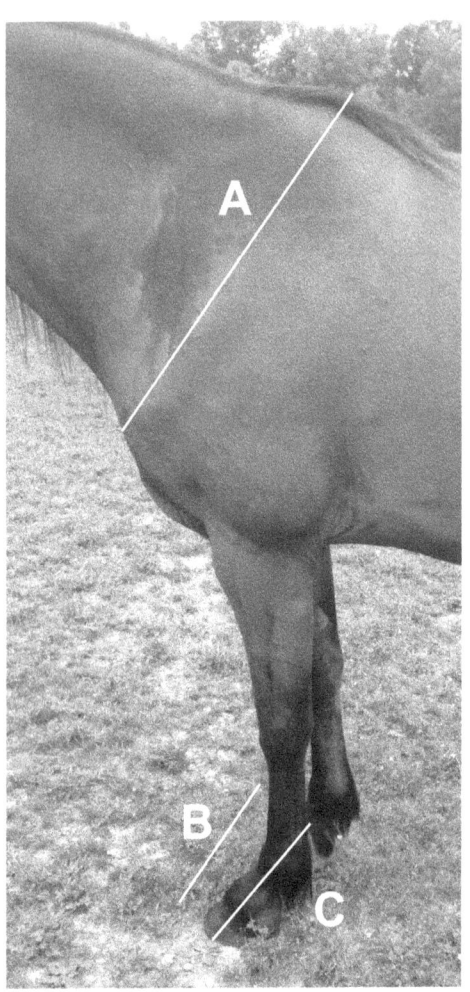

This horse's shoulder and pastern angles are nearly dead on. Lines A and B indicate the shoulder angle. Line C is the actual pastern angle.

Note that a horse with higher withers will also often have a more vertical neck, and higher action from the front legs. This is referred to as "uphill." If the hip is higher, the horse is considered "downhill." The neck of a downhill horse will most often be more

This pony's topline is clearly higher at the hip than at the withers, which gives her riders a lot of pelvic movement, but can also tip her riders forward.

level with the withers, and the stride flatter, more horizontal. The first type of conformation usually produces up and down movement at the trot (although many sport horse riders prefer an uphill horse), the second gives a lot of movement at the walk.

The second and most important consideration in your assessment of the horse's profile is the shape of the horse's middle section. In your mind's eye, draw an outline from the top of the withers to the top of the hip. Then drop the line vertically to the ground, then across the ground until it joins with a line dropped from the withers. This gives you a four-sided box, and this shape is important to the balance and movement of the horse.

In looking at your box, you will see one of three shapes: a square, a rectangle, or a tall rectangle. Some of the shapes are breed dependent. A Saddlebred, Morgan, Rocky Mountain Horse, and some sport-horse type Warmbloods tend to be tall rectangles. This means the length of the vertical lines of the box are greater than the length of the horizontal lines. These horses have very long legs!

There are exceptions, but with the tall rectangle, you often find vertical necks, a tail set high on the croup, and a lot of front end elevation in the gait. These are also the horses who can develop high-low syndrome.

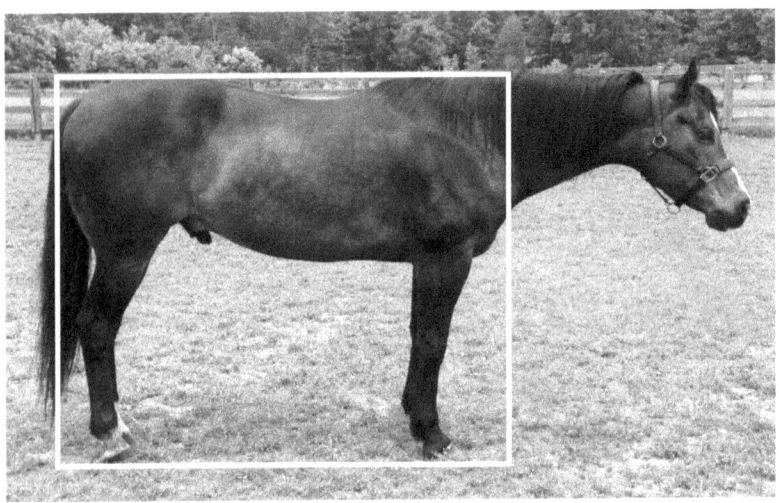

The dimensions of the white line above are 2.5 inches across and 2.06 inches down, indicating this gelding has a long topline and a rectangular shape.

Turn the tall rectangle sideways to get a horse who is longer horizontally than vertically. Many stock-type breeds have this kind of profile, and the lower neck carriage and tail set to go with it. None are either good or bad, with the exception of a very long rectangle, which means the horse has an unusually long back. This long back can be the source of soreness, and many horses with long backs need a lighter rider weight limit, as compared to a horse with a shorter back.

Some long-rectangle horses who are never ridden, or have not been ridden in a long time, still have soreness and that can become a behavioral issue, or a series of expensive and ongoing veterinary calls, massages, acupuncture treatments, and the like. It is important not to generalize, as not all horses with long backs are sore, but to take note of likelihoods and then put all the information together as a whole. Sometimes it is easier to see in a photo which profile shape a horse has.

Be sure to take in the heart girth, too, the distance between the withers and the underbelly just below the elbow. The deeper it is, the more lung capacity this horse will have when running, jumping—or going on long, challenging rides.

During your profile look, also take in the entire horse. Do all the parts seem to fit together, or does the horse have the ears of a Warmblood, neck of a Haflinger, and the legs of a Thoroughbred? Unfortunately, if the latter is the case, there are probably going to be soreness or soundness issues somewhere along the line. Some horses surprise you though, so don't assume.

20. Withers

The withers constitutes the bony protrusion at the front of the horse's back, and also ties into the neck. Some horses have very tall withers, and some have hardly any withers at all. I have even seen both extremes within the same breed, and both extremes present their own set of difficulties.

The high withered horse can be a difficult saddle fit. Here, the withers are too high to give adequate clearance for the front of the saddle. Also, the front of the saddle on a high withered horse often tips the seat of the saddle backward, causing the rider to ride out of balance with the horse. Saddles that do not fit the horse may well be the number one cause of soreness in horses. As mentioned earlier, soreness can cause behavior problems and, if left untreated, possible lameness. Think of a professional athlete

This Thoroughbred gelding has high withers, and it can be difficult to find a saddle to fit him, one that also does not tip the rider backward.

who has a sore back. Eventually he (or she) will begin to walk differently to accommodate the discomfort, and that difference in gait can put further wear and tear on other areas of the shoulders, back, hips, and legs. Ten years down the road, horse or human, the old pro has a permanent gimp in his gait.

The low withered horse can also be difficult to saddle fit, because no withers are there to hold the saddle in place. These horses often have saddles that slip from side-to-side, which is, obviously, a safety issue. A low withered horse can also become sore because it is difficult to center the saddle evenly on the horse's back. To counteract that, many people cinch or girth the horse too tightly in an attempt to keep the saddle from slipping, and that can cause pain.

The last thing to look for in the withers is even development on both the left and right sides. I have looked at several horses who had past injuries to the withers. One had somehow fallen on his back after jumping over the pasture fence and fractured his withers. In addition to having uneven withers left and right, he walked with his shoulders hunched. He was a lovely, agreeable fellow, but probably would not have held up for a lot of riding, or riding by heavy riders. I was glad to hear he found a wonderful home at a therapeutic program that allowed his great personality to shine. His new job was to help senior humans stay active, and he was groomed daily and taken for walks by people who were in their eighties.

Horses who perform the same job over a long period of time can also build muscle differently on the left and right sides of their withers. Polo and barrel racing are two sports that come to mind, as they require a horse to bend more in one direction than the other.

21. Posture

As with the horse with the broken withers, the posture of the horse is important, too. Posture is different from structure in that it is how the horse stands, versus how the horse is built. Does the horse have a dull eye, or is the tail clamped? Are the shoulders hunched? Is the neck carried lower than you might expect for a horse of his breed and conformation? Are the legs too far underneath her? Does she walk with a stride that is shorter than what you would expect?

Those are all signs of pain, and the horse's posture reflects that. I have a Jack Russell/Chihuahua mix, Abby, who was born with shallow kneecaps. While there technically is surgery to correct that, for many reasons her veterinarian felt Abby was not a good candidate.

Over time, Abby has developed an odd, wide stance behind. And, while at age twelve she still can chase a squirrel with the best, it is hard for her to raise her head and neck as high as she used to. She sometimes stands with her back bowed up, and when this happens I know she needs a puppy massage before her next session with the squirrels. Poor posture can be difficult to see in some horses, but it is always best seen in profile.

22. Barrel

The barrel of the horse covers the horse's sides, and there are two kinds: flat and round. Flat barrels are more often seen on high withered, high necked, tall rectangle horses, while rounder barrels are seen on the lower, longer horses.

It is important not to mistake fat, or lack of it, for the shape of the barrel, and sometimes feeling the horse's side is the best way to assess. The shape of the barrel is important for several reasons. First, inside the barrel is where the horse stores all of his internal organs, including his lungs. While most horses rarely need huge lung power, such as that to win a race or go on an endurance ride, the lung capacity of a horse does come into play in extreme hot or cold temperatures, or at high altitudes. The more air a horse can pump in, the more easily the horse can tolerate extremes.

For horses who will be ridden, the width the barrel provides is key. If you have difficulty with the inner thigh stretch needed to ride a draft cross, for example, then a horse with a flatter barrel will be more comfortable. If you need the stability of a broader back, however, you will find it on a horse with a wide barrel.

Most important, though, is that the horse's left and right barrel are mostly even. To look, stand ten to fifteen in front of the horse and first look at the shape of the barrel. Is the roundness (or flatness) even on both sides? For riders who prefer an even, symmetrical horse and movement, this evenness in the shape of the barrel is critical.

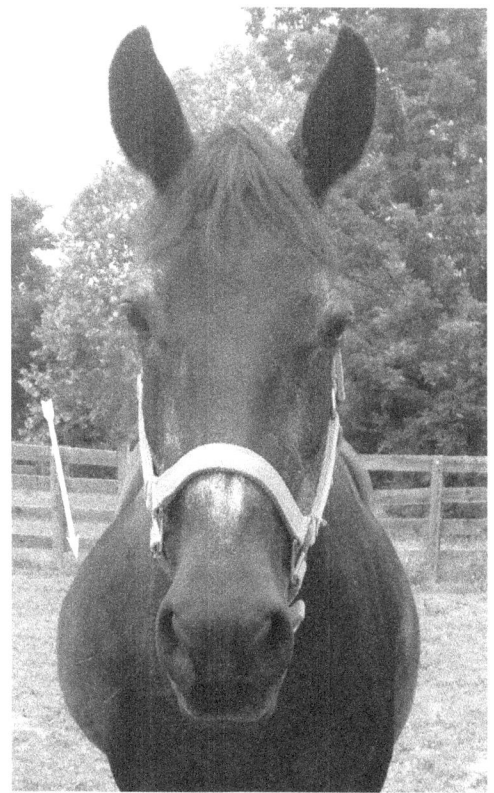

In looking at this horse's barrel, the cecal swing on the right side is apparent.

One reason both sides of the horse's barrel might not be similar is due to arthritis and/or muscle atrophy. If the horse is older, but once worked hard at polo, cutting, barrel racing, or another such sport, this might be the case. A few rubs or pats on both sides will allow you to check the area for soreness.

You might see that the right side of the horse's barrel is larger than the left. The horse stores much of her food in the cecum, which is on the right side of her body. When the horse has eaten a lot of hay, the right side of her barrel may bulge outward and when she walks toward you, you will see a large left to right swing of her belly. This is called the cecal swing.

Depending on what the horse ate, or didn't eat, before you arrived, you may not see much of a swing. Some horses have a huge cecal swing, while others, even with a belly full of hay, do not have much at all.

Regardless of the cause, an uneven barrel can put unbalanced riders even more off balance. If the rider's left leg drops vertically on a flat barreled horse, but the right leg has to spread outward at the hip to accommodate a large cecal swing, or more muscle tone on the right side, the horse might not be a suitable mount.

23. Stomach

Like the profile, the horse's stomach is best viewed from the side. Ideally, you will see a nice straight line from the horse's elbow to where the underside of the belly ties into the gaskin. That is the sign of a nice, healthy, horse—and one who is fit. If the belly dips downward, the horse you are looking at might be out of shape, or over-weight. Sometimes it is hard to see past a big, drooping hay belly, which will

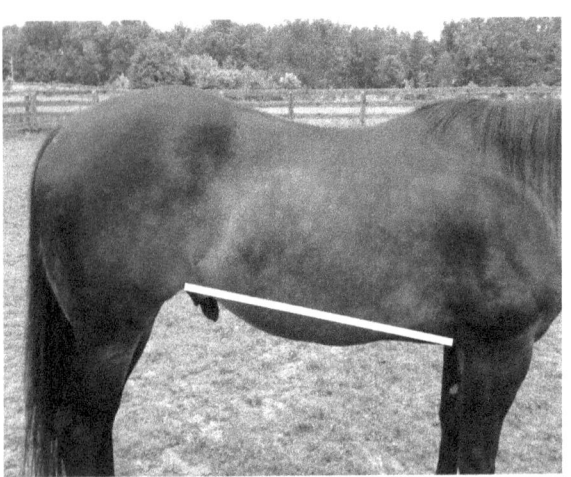

While not in top physical condition, the belly line on this gelding shows him to be relatively fit and of appropriate weight.

go away with diet, and good quality hay and exercise.

Worms can also cause a hay belly, and a look around the horse's living space to see if manure is left to pile up will give an indication if this is a cause. A bony topline and dull hair coat might confirm your suspicions. This is a good reason to have the horse's vet records available during your visit. In the past, veterinarians did a lot of the worming, but today, with improvements in medications and products, most equine caregivers take charge of the worming themselves. You might, however, see on the record if the vet has wormed the horse, or made note of the product the owner used, and when.

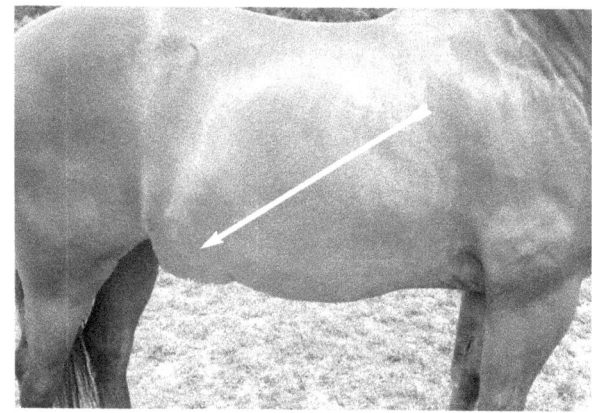

Horses of all breeds and ages can get a hernia. Some will limit a horse's activity, some not.

A final cause of a low belly might be a hernia. Horses of all breeds and ages can get a hernia, and there are many causes, including genetics, overwork, and injury. Often, but not always, the hernia is seen toward the back of the belly as an uneven bulge. Some hernias require costly surgery, while others heal on their own.

24. Back

As a general rule, the horse's back, loin, and croup (the distance from the highest point of the withers to the top of the tail) should

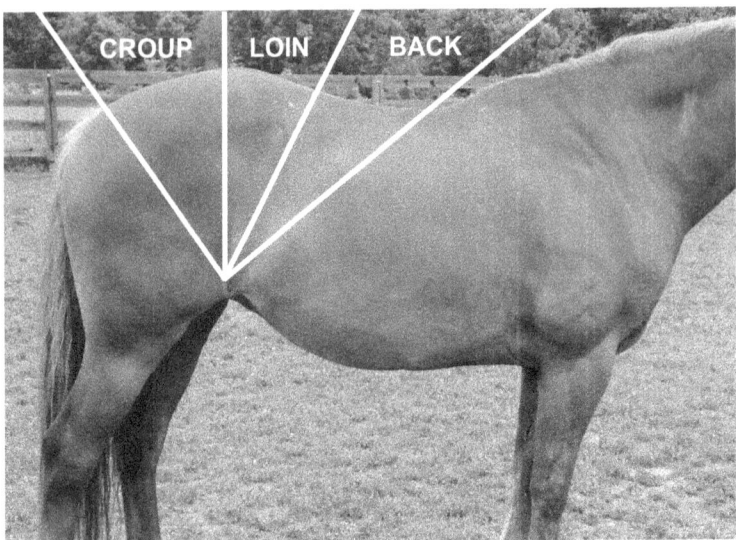

This horse is a little long in the croup, as compared to the back and loin. The length of the croup is important because it is the "engine" that powers the horse. A long croup also houses more muscle mass. Many horses are long in the back or loin and short in the croup, which weakens the horse's rear power pack.

be about equal in length. Horses with long backs and short loins are seen more often than the other way around and the problem with that is a long back can be a weak back. If the horse is to be ridden, a weak back means the horse can carry less weight than a shorter backed horse of the same size, age, and condition. A long back also makes it harder for the horse to round out her back to engage her hindquarters for collection. And, a long back is more prone to muscular strain, especially as the horse ages.

On the plus side, a longer back can be more flexible, and the movement given by a long back can provide a smooth ride.

In addition to the length of the back, also note how level it is. An older, long backed horse might be sway backed. When the center of the back drops, it becomes difficult to find a saddle that fits. What usually happens then is that the weight of the saddle and rider bridges (or opens up a gap) in the low center of the horse's back and only puts weight where the front and back of the saddle touch the horse. This causes soreness, which can result in behavior problems. No one, horse or human, likes to work when they hurt.

Finally, look for adequate padding over the entire backbone. If the backbone is raised, it could be that the horse is thin, and needs to gain weight. Or, you could be looking at muscle atrophy. That important layer of fat padding lying along the spine is not all fat. Instead, it is muscle that helps each horse move forward and support the rider, so it is important that there be enough of it.

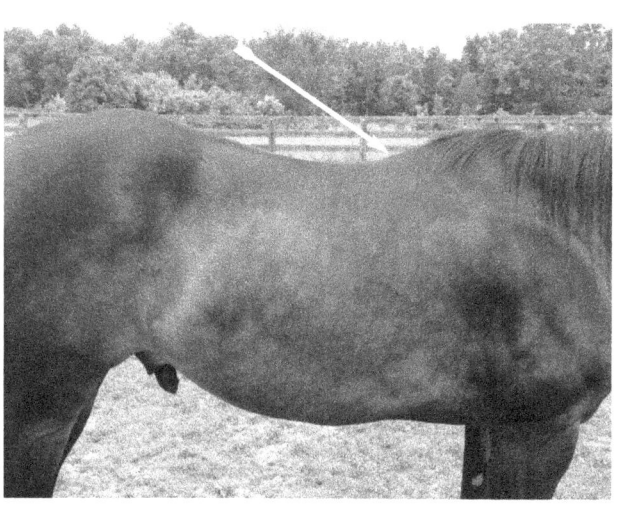

At nineteen, this horse's back has dropped over the past few years. Without some strengthening exercises, within a few years it will most likely drop even more.

That muscle helps the horse "use" her back effectively. Some horses, however, such as big, rangy, Thoroughbreds, always seem to have a protruding backbone and are just fine for many purposes. It is just one other area for you to consider.

25. Loin

The loin is the area between the horse's lower ribs and pelvis, and is where the lumbar vertebrae are located. As with the back, it should be roughly one third of the distance from the withers to the top of the tail. Most horses have six lumbar vertebrae, but some breeds, such as the Arabian, have five. Regardless of the number, they are the largest of the horse's vertebrae.

The loin connects the horse's hindquarters and front end together. This is where all the power from the hindquarters transfers to the front when the horse moves. The loin should be strong and muscled, so a special concern would be if the horse is sore in this area. Often the back of a saddle, especially a western saddle with a rolled edge, can dig into the horse's loin and be quite painful. If the loin is weak or sore, the horse will have a difficult, painful time supporting the weight of a rider.

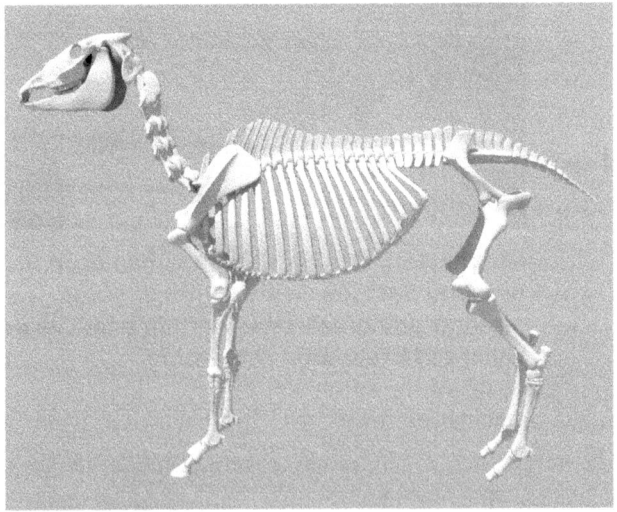

The horse does not have a single back "bone," but instead has many spiky vertical "fingers" of bone called the spinous processes.

26. Croup

Along with the back and loin, the croup is the final of the "thirds," and should be about equal in length to the first two.

Depending on the breed of your horse, the croup may be flat or sloped. Arabians, Standardbreds, Walking Horses and other breeds with a narrow build and high neck carriage often have a flatter croup.

The croup should be uniform in width, muscular, and even across the top. The length of the croup is associated with speed and endurance, while the width is associated with strength or power.

Horses with flatter croups are often good jumpers, as they have a long stride and can get their hind legs way out behind them, so as to get over a tall fence. Those with more slope to the croup, such as the Quarter Horse, can get their hind legs underneath and push off with great power in many short strides for short bursts of speed. But, a croup that is too steep can indicate weak hips and hocks.

27. Rear Legs (overview)

As with the front legs, you should be able to drop a vertical line from the top of the back leg, down the cannon bone and through the center of the back of the foot to the ground. In many horses, the stifles are canted slightly outward, which puts the hocks slightly inward. This allows the horse to more easily move her back legs, and it should not be considered much of a conformational fault.

Horses can also stand base-wide and base-narrow in the rear, just as they can in the front. A horse who is base-narrow behind can also be bowlegged, and over time, this can cause soreness or unsoundness. Additionally, and as with the front feet, hind toes can point left or right, instead of straight ahead, and any of these derivative stances can cause arthritis.

28. Hip

The hip refers to a line running from the tuber coxae (the point of the hip) to the ischium (the point of the buttock). The key factor here is that the points of the hips should be even. To determine this, stand well behind the horse. Be sure all four of the horse's feet are placed squarely underneath him, then find the point of the left and right hips. This is the bony protrusion you see on each side of the horse.

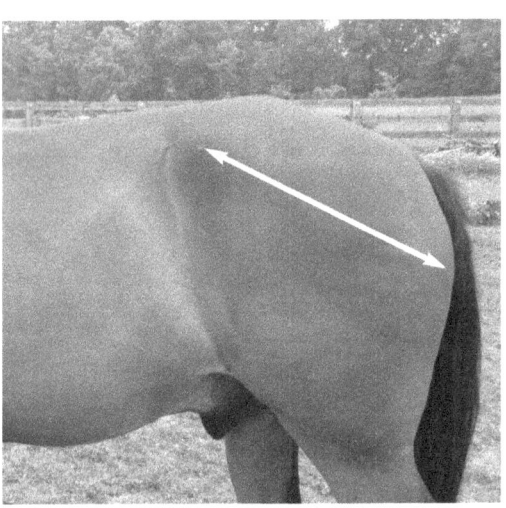

The tuber coxae and ischium.

On a big, heavy horse this may be harder to see, but maybe a friend or the horse's owner can help. Have one person stand on each side of the horse, and place his or her index finger on the point of the horse's hip. Each point should be an equal distance from the ground. If one hip is higher than the other, think arthritis, old injury, or a decreased range of motion on one side. If a hip is dropped, it will be harder for the horse to reach that back leg fully under himself, causing a deviation to his natural gait.

Uneven hips provide uneven movement for the rider. The trot or gaited movement will be dissimilar behind, and the horse may canter or lope without one or both back legs reaching underneath his belly. If an even, continuous, symmetrical gait is important to you, this horse will not be able to provide it. Only your veterinarian or equine chiropractor can tell you the extent of the situation—and if it can be remedied.

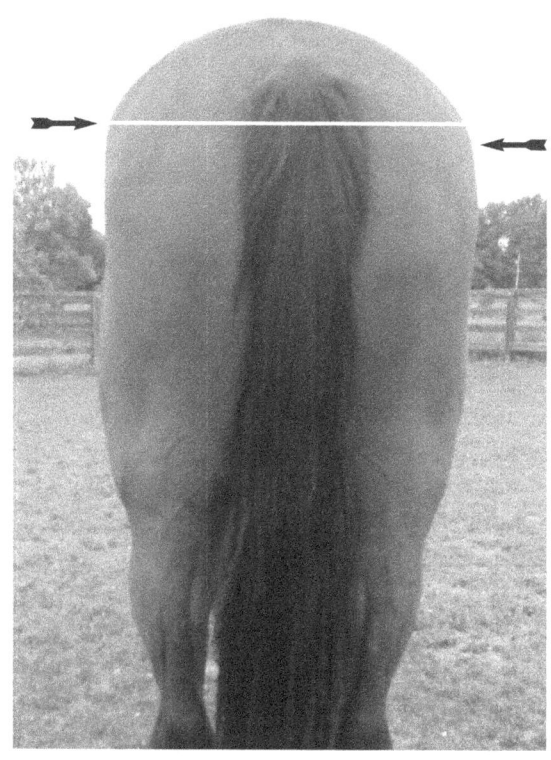

This horse's left hip is a little higher than his right.

Now, from the side, look at the angle of the hip, and also the angle of the shoulder. The two angles should be a reverse match of each other. Horses who have matching angles here seem to be more athletic, have a better chance at staying sound, and have the ability to collect easily. Remember, too, that this degree of angle should match, or be close to, the angle of the front pasterns.

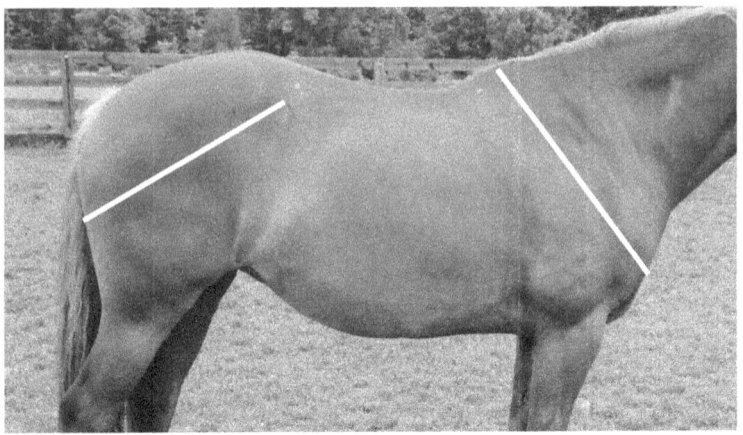

The shoulder here is at a steeper angle than the hip. This mare has a choppy trot, but provides a lot of rider pelvic movement at the walk.

29. Stifle

While the front legs bear most of the weight of the horse, it's the back legs that provide the power for the horse to move forward. Before looking at your prospective horse's back legs, it is important to understand some of the structure of the leg. The horse's back leg starts at the stifle, which is the joint nearest the line of the belly, and is also the largest single joint in the horse's body. It is the equivalent of the human knee, and like the knee, helps the horse's hind leg stay firmly planted on the ground.

Because the stifle is also the most complicated joint in the horse's body, with many bones being similar to a human knee, it is an area prone to injury. Activities that involve quick speed and direction changes—such as jumping, roping, cutting, polo, and barrel racing—can cause trauma to the stifle. So if this horse does, or has done, any of these activities regularly, pay special attention to discomfort in this area.

30. Hock

Moving down the leg, the next joint is the hock, which is similar to the human ankle, with the point of the hock correlating to the human heel.

From the side, your horse's hocks should be clean, with no swelling or scar tissue. A capped hock, or bursitis of the hock, is the result of an injury and is noticed by a swelling at the end of the hock. This swelling may or may not be permanent, and there may or may not be lameness associated with it. A capped hock is relatively common as injuries go, and something to both look for and consider.

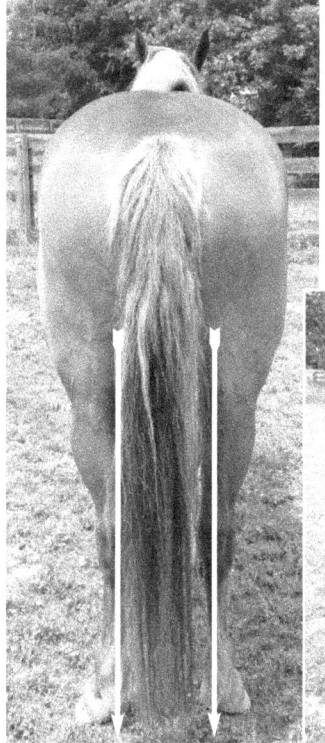

This Belgian cross (left), like many draft horses, is cow hocked. For generations, draft horses were bred that way so they could step in the ploughed furrows without breaking them up. The horse directly below is structurally better, with the line dropping straight through the hock, cannon bone, and the back of the hoof.

The hock also helps propel the horse forward, and sports that put a lot of twist on the hock, such as cutting, polo, and reining, can over time cause arthritis, or weakness in this joint. As with the front legs, when standing behind the horse, you should be able to drop a vertical line from the top of the leg, through the center of the hock and cannon bone, down through the back of the hoof.

From the side, you should also be able to drop a vertical line from the point of the horse's buttock to the top of the hock and down to the back of the fetlock. Horses who fulfill this measurement, or come close, can carry weight well and also reach under him- or herself to propel forward.

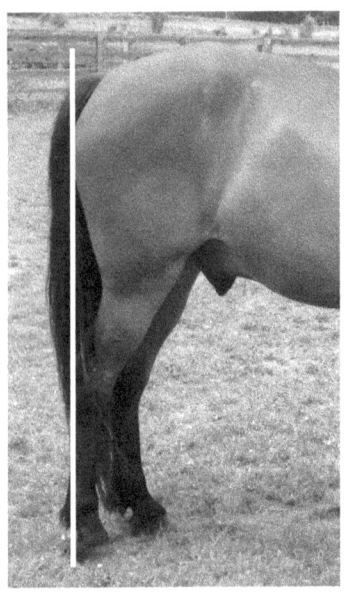

This Walking Horse can reach well underneath, and overtracks well.

Some proponents of horse sports, such as reining, like a horse who is a little cow hocked, thinking it makes it easier for the horse to slide and make quick turns. In addition, many draft horses were bred to be cow hocked, so they could use their back legs more freely to help them pull heavy loads.

A cousin to cow-hocked conformation is sickle-hocked. This is where the angle of the hock, from the side, is deep. A sickle-hocked horse will normally stand with his rear legs farther underneath him than the average horse, and the condition can put stress on the cannon bone and back of the hock.

The opposite of sickle-hocked is straight-hocked, or hocks that are too straight. In older horses, you might see stifle soreness, suspensory issues, or arthritis in the hock, if it is too straight. These horses usually hold up better than horses who are sickle hocked, but hocks that are somewhere in the middle are best.

In looking at your prospective horse, keep in mind what you need the horse to do. Every horse will have some deviation from these guidelines, but extreme deviation may mean an unsoundness or extra expense to keep the horse comfortable.

31. Rear Pastern and Fetlock

The rear pastern is, like the front, a shock absorber, but because most of the horse's weight is carried on the front legs, the angle of the rear pastern should be a little steeper than in the front. This steepness adds strength to the joint. As with the front pasterns, this area can develop ringbone or sidebone, and can also feature a host of other interesting lumps that may or may not be painful to the horse when you touch them, or when he moves.

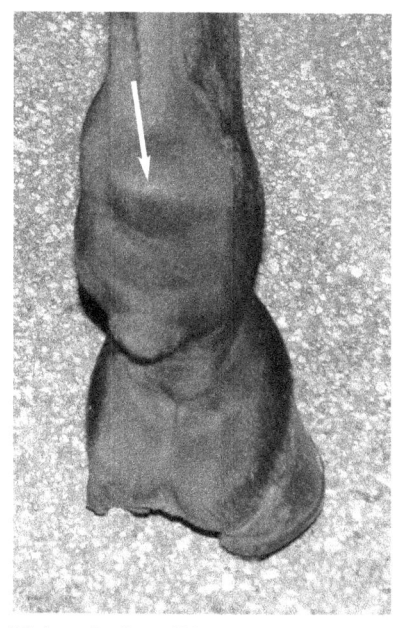

Scars on the back of the pastern are a concern, as there is an intricate set of tendon and ligament support structures that can be hampered by scar tissue. Some scars in this area can impede movement, or cause pain.

The fetlock is a stabilizer of the lower limb, so it must be healthy, flexible, and strong.

This wind puff is on the back of the fetlock, but causes the horse no pain or loss of range of motion.

32. Tail

The horse's tail serves many purposes. In addition to being an excellent fly swatter, it is a communication tool, windbreak, protection device, and helps balance the horse. If you are in a cold or windy climate, a long, thick tail keeps wind and cold from racing between the horse's back legs and to the underside of the horse's body, where hair often is not as thick. Ever hear the old adage about a horse turning his tail to the wind? That's why.

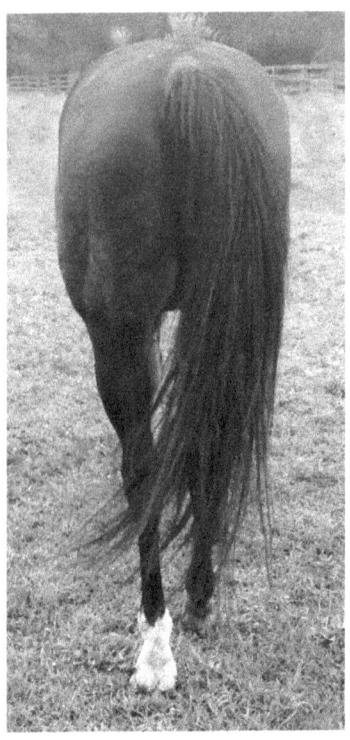

A tail held to one side may indicate pain.

The tail is also part of the horse's spinal column and can be a good indicator of soundness or soreness. First, stand well behind the horse when he is standing square on all four feet. Is the tail carried loosely and evenly between the horse's butt cheeks? Or, is the top of the tail cocked to one side?

Next, watch the horse's tail as he walks straight away from you. Is the tail still loose and even, or is it held to one side? If the horse carries his tail to the left or right, there may be soreness or arthritis over the lumbar vertebrae, hips, or even farther up the back. Often, the issue becomes more prominent with movement. But, you won't know how severe the issue is until you get an equine medical professional in to evaluate. The problem should be noted, though.

Often a cocked tail is just minor soreness and can be worked out with massage, acupuncture, or chiropractic adjustments. If the cocked tail has been left untreated for many months, or years, then arthritis may have developed, which will be harder to manage.

As mentioned, the tail is an important tool in balance. The horse will move his tail left or right to round corners or counteract the weight of an unbalanced rider. So, if the horse has limited movement in his tail, trotting balanced around a corner or carrying an unwieldy rider could be difficult.

If you feel safe doing so, grab the tail about eight inches from the base, and give it a gentle shake. The tail should shake freely and feel loose in your hand. Unless, of course, the horse takes issue with you and clamps her tail down tight to her butt cheeks. She may just feel she doesn't know you well enough yet!

Minus any clamping, if the tail is resistant to movement, this can be yet another indication of soreness somewhere in the horse's body. As you continue to assess the entire horse, keep an eye on his tail, as he will communicate to you with it. Every swish, clamp, or up and down flap means something, even if he is just telling a fly to get lost.

33. Muscle Tone

While not a traditional part of the build of the horse, the muscle tone and amount of muscle on the horse is important, too. A well-muscled horse is an indication of good health, as well as the ability to be physically active. Some stock-type horses and draft or draft crosses have a large amount of heavy, bulky muscle. These are often strong horses with wide backs. Arabians, the Hackney Pony, and other such breeds are lighter muscled and can, as a whole, move very quickly.

Whichever kind of muscle the horse has, it is important that it be evenly distributed on both the left and right sides of the horse. It seems as though it would be, but there are many instances where that is not the case.

Older horses who have been mounted from the ground their entire lives often have different muscling on the left and right sides of their shoulders, back, and barrel. This is because, for years, the horse had to brace for the twisting motion of the saddle that accompanied a mount from the ground. Over time, the horse then built asymmetrical musculature. This can make it difficult to find a saddle to fit the different sides of the horse, and can cause misalignment in the bones of the back, as well as arthritis.

In addition, as mentioned earlier, horses who are involved in activities that require the performance of the same moves over and over can also develop differently from left side to right. Polo ponies are a good example. In polo, the rider usually swings the mallet from the right side of the horse. As a protective measure the horse begins to move with his head, neck, and hips canted to the left. This is to reduce the chance that the horse might mistakenly be hit with the mallet. Over time, the horse begins to move with a decided curve to the left and builds up different muscle tone on the left and right sides of the body. From experience, it is a time consuming process to get a seasoned polo pony to walk with their head and hips straight. Some, due to arthritis and atrophy, will always be dissimilar left and right in both their movement and their muscle tone.

That said, retired polo ponies typically make great therapy, 4-H, and trail horses. They have experienced so much that they are generally unflappable, get along well in the herd, and are willing and easy-going. Physical issues aside, I look very closely at any polo pony, for there is usually a lot of good there.

Two other sports that can make a horse develop differently are barrel racing (more left turns than right) and roping, as there is some of the same left twist to the head and neck as with the polo horses, due to the right-hand throw of the rope.

34. Scars and Blemishes

Scars and blemishes may be unsightly, but they are not necessarily harmful to the horse's soundness or well-being. The difference between the two is simple. A scar is the leftover of an accident to the skin or underlying soft tissue, and may or may not be deep or involve surrounding areas. A blemish is the result of an injury, poor conformation, or overuse that results in a lump or disfigurement, large or small, usually near joints or on the long bones of the legs.

In looking at scars, the location often determines if there will be a serious effect on the horse. First, look for a big, noticeable scar. The owner may be able to tell you about it, how it got there, and how long ago. Then run your hands over the horse's body to find smaller scars and blemishes, such as warts, or some other

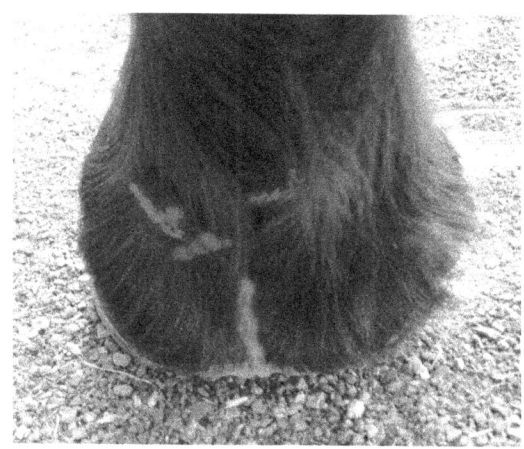

Even though these scars are more than a decade old, the original injury was enough to make this front hoof different in size and shape from the other front hoof. This horse is often gimpy when barefoot, but does fine with a set of front shoes.

lump. Some of these can be covered by the horse's hair, especially in colder months. The running of your hands also accomplishes another purpose, that of checking the horse for soreness.

If you find a scar on a joint, or in a location that would be covered by a girth, saddle, or bridle, pay special attention. I once worked with a horse who developed a large wart under his belly near his front legs, right where the girth went. He was pleasant at some times, and cranky at others. We finally realized the wart was there and, depending on which girth was used, he sometimes was uncomfortable when saddled. The wart was easily removed, though, and once he healed he was fine. Scars over a joint, if severe enough, can cause intermittent, or even permanent, unsoundness.

A blemish, in turn, can be a fluid filled lump, such as a wind puff (usually caused by poor conformation, injury, or overuse), capped elbow (often caused by a horse knocking his elbow with a front shoe when lying down), or a harder lump, such as a splint. Or, a blemish can be a potentially serious injury such as a bowed tendon, as long as the horse is sound. Blemishes usually do not interfere with riding, although they are frowned upon in many show pens, especially in conformation or halter classes.

One other kind of blemish to look for is a divot, or indentation, in the skin. I've seen these on the horse's face, neck, flank, as well as other areas. The divot may be part of a scar, but it can also have been caused by trauma, such as a kick from another horse. In rare instances, it can indicate neurological damage.

35. Skin and Hair

The next areas to check are the skin and hair. These are two other areas that closely tie into conformation, because a flaw in the skin or hair can be considered a blemish, or even an unsoundness.

The skin is more important than it looks, as it protects the inside of the horse's body from rain, wind, dirt, and all sorts of contamination, and also helps maintain the horse's internal body temperature.

With a quick spot check, using your fingers to part the hair, look for scaly patches or open sores. Poor skin can be an indication

This mare loses the chestnut hair on her face in the summer, as seen by her bare nose, and continuing above the noseband of her halter.

of many things, including flies, poor nutrition, or lack of grooming. These are simple matters to correct, however, worms, fungus, allergies, liver disease, or other illness that causes skin problems may require more intensive work to remedy.

In the summer, some chestnut horses lose the hair on their faces. This can be a reaction to their own sweat that resolves itself once the temperature cools down. This also is where the blemish and unsoundness part comes into play. Does the issue interfere with the horse's normal functioning or intended purpose?

Some horses, especially white and gray horses, are prone to melanomas, which may or may not be malignant. These tumors can appear as spots or patches, or raised or flat masses. Most have a dark surface, and can cluster around the eye, or the base of the tail. Depending on the location of the tumor, it can be a simple blemish, or it can restrict sight or movement and cause an unsoundness.

It is easy to understand that a nice, glossy coat of hair is a sign of a healthy horse. Fortunately, most horses have this; it is the horses who don't that you need to look at more closely. If the horse is missing patches of hair, he or she may be low on the totem pole and be regularly picked on by other members of the herd. Or, the horse could have an allergy and be scratching the hair away. Gnats could be an issue, too, as they can cause patchy hair loss in the summer. Lice, mange, urine or manure scald, rain scald, ringworm (which is a fungus), too much selenium, or even sarcoid skin tumors can also cause hair loss.

Sarcoids usually affect younger horses, but can be infective from one horse to the other. If you suspect that your horse prospect has these, do not bring the horse onto your property until a veterinarian has given the horse the all clear. Most of the other conditions mentioned are simple environmental fixes.

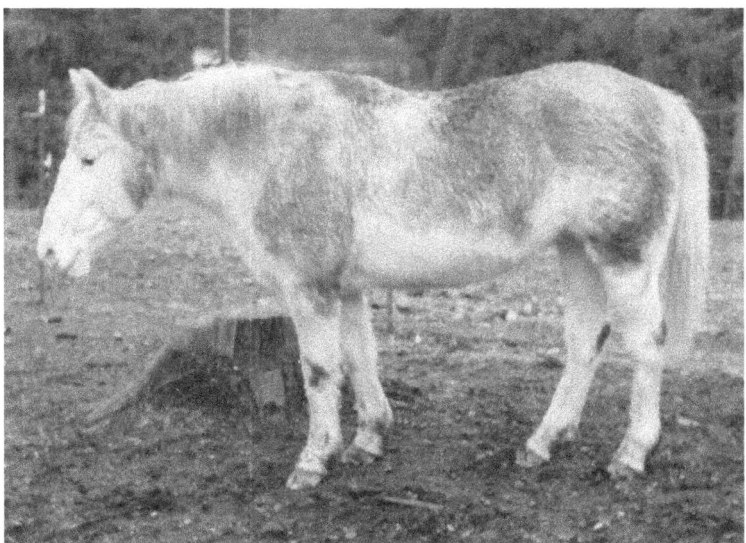

This mud-loving old girl has developed Cushings, as seen by the long hair. Also, under the mud are lumpy fat patches.

What about dull, coarse hair? Think poor nutrition, or nutrition that is out of balance with regard to fats, carbohydrates, and/or proteins. Parasites or a systemic infection also come to mind in horses with a dull hair coat. Allergies or hormones could factor in, too.

If the horse's hair is exceptionally long and it is not the middle of winter, Cushings could be the cause. The Cushinoid horse may still make an excellent horse for you, but will need special care, including a dry lot as grasses can, in some cases, be deadly.

36. Weight

Like people, some horses by nature are thinner or heavier. We have a Thoroughbred at Colby's Army who is always on the lean side, no matter how many quality calories we stuff into him. On the other hand, Haflingers, Fjords, and some pony breeds always seem to be on the heavy side. It's as if they gain weight on the air they breathe.

A horse's weight comes into play during an assessment if the horse is overly fat or thin. Thank goodness that heavier horses are more common than thin ones, but those who are heavy might not be so from too much food. In addition to Cushings, hormones, breed type, or lack of exercise may be a factor. If a horse is overly fat, it also makes it more difficult to assess his or her conformation, as many of the angles can get buried in all of the plumpness.

If it looks as if the very thin horse has adequate feed, there could be many variables that keep the horse from gaining weight. Hormones make this list, too, as do parasites, systemic infection, gastric ulcers, stress, and breed type. But, dental issues top the list.

A horse has to chew food thoroughly if he is to digest it completely. If his teeth have been neglected, he might not be able to chew properly. A sharp point on a tooth, a tooth that is infected, or an oral abscess can cause discomfort and make a horse hesitant to eat. Only an equine dentist or DVM can let you know for sure if this horse has a dental problem.

Just like you, if a horse's teeth hurt, he may adjust his gait so as not to jar the tooth into more pain. This adjustment will then translate into many areas of your assessment, including posture, soreness (because the adjustment in gait is sure to cause at least a few sore areas across his body), and flexibility, to name a few possibilities.

37. Size and Build

The size and build of the horse matters a great deal, and for several reasons. One is pertinent to showing. If a registered horse is above or below the breed's allowed height range, you will have difficulty entering any breed classes. Another is breed type. I once worked with a registered Saddlebred mare who, from the withers back, looked more like a ranch-bred Quarter Horse. If you plan to compete in breed shows, your horse should be built somewhat close to the breed standard.

Then, the horse's weight determines the size of the rider. Of course, the horse's age, conformation, general health, and level of conditioning also have to be considered. It is understandable that a horse cannot carry as much weight at age twenty as he did when he was seven, but the horse will let you know if his weight load is too high. If he is cranky and you suspect his current rider is on the heavy side, maybe his mood will improve after a few short weeks of rest.

Rider weight can be a touchy subject to bring up to a seller, though, and is sometimes best left alone. Following are additional guidelines if the amount of weight the horse will be expected to carry is a concern:

- Choose a horse with big cannon bones, wide loins, and a short back
- Avoid heavy saddles
- Ride with good posture and balance
- Make sure the saddle fits the horse really well

A few words on driving and vaulting, as these sports are growing in popularity. The average healthy, well-conformed horse can pull his own weight, but that is conditional upon having a cart or carriage with well-maintained axles and wheels. You must also consider how deep the footing is, the age and fitness of the horse, how long you ask the horse to pull, the weight of the driver(s) and the size of the wheels on the cart. When you change conditions, such as adding hills or sand, or a lot of moisture into the ground, you lower the amount of weight the horse can pull.

Many people choose to drive ponies or small horses, even miniature horses, and this can be a lot of fun, as long as you keep in mind the weight each small horse can physically pull.

Vaulting horses tend to be tall, with wide backs, lots of bone, good left and right symmetry, and an even, rhythmic stride at the walk, trot, and canter. Warmbloods and smaller drafts can do well here, as can draft crosses or wide Appaloosas, Quarter Horses, and Paints. Vaulting horses must, obviously, be very strong across their back, loin and croup, with no discernable soreness.

38. Range of Motion (overview)

Now that you've assessed various aspects of the horse's body, you will need to see how well they actually work. This is a good way to see how your initial conformation assessments match up to reality. Often, horses surprise me. One can present with relatively good conformation and no noticeable soreness, and yet still be stiff as a board. Or, vice versa.

Flexibility is the key to a strong, well-balanced horse. Any athlete knows the benefit of stretching, bending, and flexing to improve strength and performance, and no matter what the two of you do together, your horse is definitely an athlete. The range of motion the horse has, or, how flexible he or she is, will tell you volumes about the condition of the horse's muscular and skeletal systems.

If the horse can flex to one side but not the other, he could be uncomfortable when performing both mounted and unmounted tasks. Chiropractic, massage, or acupuncture may—or may not—be able to help. If he flexes very little in either direction, you may be looking at ongoing pain management. Only a qualified equine medical professional can say for sure.

Following are a few moves and stretches that will give a good idea of where this particular horse is with regard to movement.

39. Head and Neck Stretch

The poll is a control center for the mechanics of the horse's body, and several nerves in this area control the proprioception of the horse. This is where signals from nerves trigger the horse's muscles and skeleton to move a certain way. Many people don't realize how significantly this area of the horse's body governs the horse's way of going. The flexibility of the neck really does determine the flexibility of the body. So, a tight poll indicates a tight horse. A loose, supple poll, one that flexes both from side-to-side and up and down, creates loose, fluid movement throughout the horse's body.

When it comes to riding, it is all about the movement of the horse. If the horse cannot move properly, the rider loses out. Earlier, you checked to see if the horse's poll was sore. This first stretch tests the horse's ability to move his poll and neck from side-to-side by gently bringing the nose back to the shoulder. There are two ways to do this.

In the first method, stand to the horse's left (a foot or so from the horse's ear) and face the horse. Bring your left hand to the right of the horse's muzzle, and gently apply pressure to encourage the horse to bring his nose around, toward you, to his left shoulder. You may need to help by applying gentle pressure with your right hand to the left side of the horse's neck or shoulder. The goal is to do this while the horse's legs stay planted squarely underneath him. If the horse swings his rear to the right, instead of bending, stand the horse with a fence or wall next to his right side.

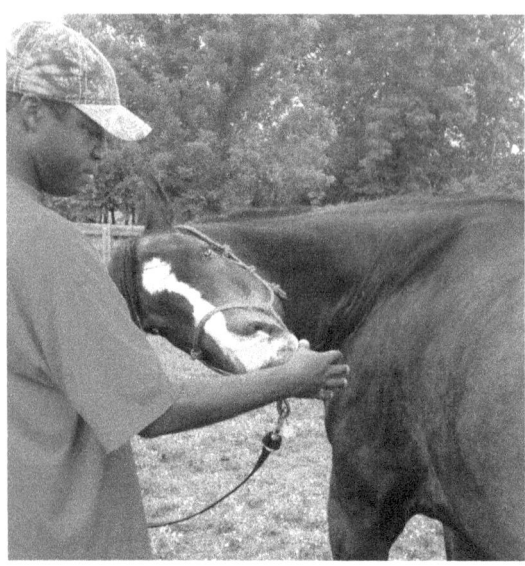

This horse shows great range of motion as he chases a carrot back to his shoulder. He was equally as limber to his right.

You may prefer the second method, but will need the owner's permission, especially if the horse has foundered or has Cushings and is on a "no treat" diet. Here, you will stand to the left of the horse's shoulder, and hold a carrot or other treat to the left of the horse's muzzle. Then bring the treat back to the horse's shoulder to see how hard the horse has to work to get it.

With either method, as you go through the process, you will get a sense of how easy or difficult it is for the horse to complete this movement. A younger horse should have no trouble doing this move on either side, but an older horse may have more trouble on one side than the other.

During the conformation assessment, did you note any scars or structural issues that might prohibit this horse from having good flexion? It is always interesting to see if your early thoughts translate into facts.

40. Nose to Chest Stretch

The nose to chest stretch tests the ability of the horse to loosen his poll up and down. Again, a carrot or treat is helpful, if the owner approves. Simply hold the treat below the horse's muzzle, and then bring it to the horse's chest.

If she does well, try again, but this time move the treat lower, to between the horse's legs at the girth area. The horse should access the treat from between her front legs, not by going around the shoulder at the side.

Remember that under the direction of a veterinarian or even a massage therapist, these moves and stretches can sometimes be good daily physical fitness for your horses. Today they are simply assessments.

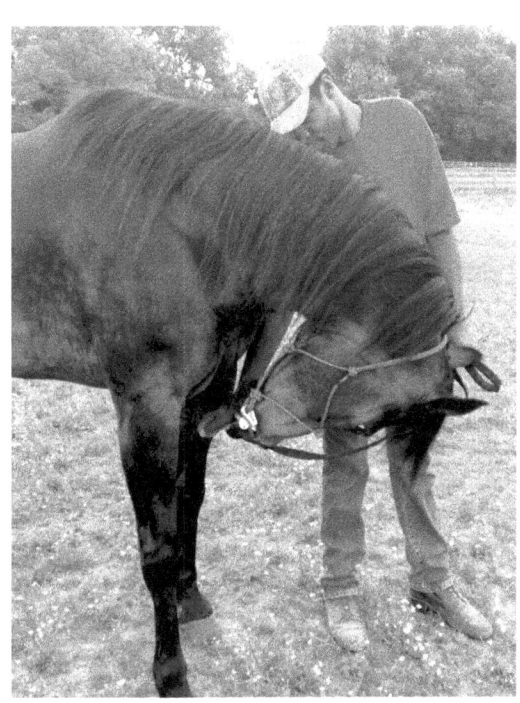

On his way to between his front legs. There is no trouble in this horse's poll.

41. Front Leg Stretch

Leg stretches give an indication of soundness and range of motion in the limb. If for example, the prospective horse has good range of motion on the left front and stretches well there, but does not want to comply when asked to do the same with the right front leg, the horse could be sore. Or, arthritis or muscle atrophy could limit the horse's range of motion. Remember, too, that a leg stretch also involves muscles in the horse's shoulder and back, and that any limited range of motion might originate there, rather than in the leg itself.

The horse's motion is one key component that helps the rider. Limit the motion; limit the rider's ability to balance, and to help the horse collect or extend. It is good to note here that ideally, the horse's movement needs to be equal on both sides and freely given, no matter what his or her natural stride. If a sore horse shortens his natural stride by six inches, it becomes an unnatural movement for that horse and translates to stiffness and tenseness throughout the horse's back and body. That stiff movement can then be jolting to the rider.

There is some conversation about whether to try this next stretch after the horse has been standing for a while, or if the horse should be walked first. This would be a good time to defer to the owner's wishes.

First, pick up the front leg as you would to pick out the hoof. Note the angle of the shoulder, and stretch the front leg out in front of the horse at the same angle as the shoulder. Be sure to hold the leg with one hand under the knee and the other at the hoof. The hoof should stay low to the ground. If you raise the hoof too high, you may stress joints, muscles, ligaments or tendons. If the horse resists, do not pull against him. All you need to see is if this position is comfortable, or not.

Next, move the leg back to see how far ahead of the hind foot you can place the front. Most horses cannot stretch all the way back, but see how far the horse can reach. Again, keep the foot low to the ground to avoid stress.

You can also wiggle the limb from side-to-side, keeping in mind that you are not there to actually stretch the horse, but rather to see how far his limbs will easily move. Make note of all three ranges of motion on the left side—front, back, and side-to-side—and then do the same on the right side to compare.

Do the actual stretches match up to what you first saw? Did the leg with the scar tissue seem more resistant? Was the leg with the outward-facing hoof more difficult to move side-to-side? Be sure to take good notes, so you can refer to them later.

42. Back Leg Stretch

As with other parts of the horse, there are many stretches that can be done with the back (or hind) legs, and each stretch accomplishes different goals. But, remember that the stretches you will use for evaluation are simple range of motion stretches for the purpose of assessment. This is not the time to ask the horse to stretch beyond what is comfortable.

First, start by picking up a hind leg as if you were going to pick out the hoof, then gently extend the leg back and down. You will not actually stretch the leg here, just see how

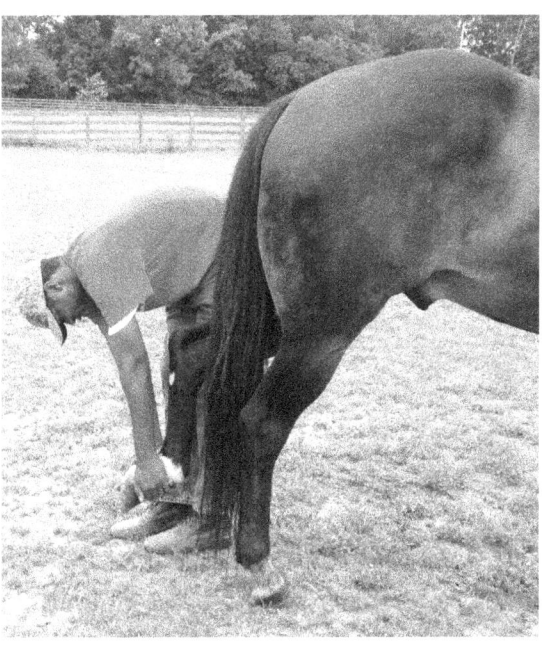

A lot of resistance was met when trying to extend the back leg. This was as far as the horse was comfortable going.

far back you can get it to extend. Sometimes the horse will stretch his leg back on his own, and that is a good sign.

In the second stretch, hold the fetlock with one hand, and with your other hand, support the leg above the hock. Gently try to bring the hind leg forward, to just behind the front leg. Many horses cannot reach that far, but see how far you get. Again, be sure to keep the foot low to the ground. This is to avoid stress on the horse's soft tissue.

The third and last stretch is a diagonal hind leg stretch. Here, if you feel safe doing so, pick up the right hind leg from the left side, by reaching under the horse's belly. Then gently place the right hind behind the left front.

Do each stretch from both sides. What you are looking for is not how far you can move each leg, although that is important, too, but that the horse can move his hind legs equally well on both sides of his body. If you notice that one side moves significantly farther than the other, the horse might not be the best candidate for you, especially if you will be asking a lot physically from your horse.

On the other hand, if you will just be doing the occasional, short, slow weekend trail ride, this horse might become your new best friend. The intended purpose for the horse really comes into play here.

Overall, age makes a big difference in a horse's flexibility and that should be taken into consideration as you write down your comments. The average six-year-old horse will have more flex than a sixteen-year-old. In addition, your assessment is not about pushing the horse out of his or her comfort zone, but in finding what range of motion is easily reached.

43. Belly Lift

When the horse is asked to raise his belly, it is as if he is asked to do a standing collection. When asked to collect under saddle, the horse has to raise his belly and lift his spine to make that happen. This next move tests the ability of the horse to tighten his abdominal muscles, much as a human would do a sit up.

The importance of strong abdominal muscles translates directly to the strength of a horse's back, which correlates to rider weight—and to the amount of weight a horse can pull.

There are several ways to ask a horse to lift his belly, but the simplest is to have one person hold the horse while you use the tips of your fingers to put upward pressure on the horse's belly just behind the girth area. Both people should note any movement

This mare's ear shows she is aware of her human partner. She also was able to lift her belly quite a bit.

when pressure is applied. The person who holds the horse can see movement, while you, while applying the pressure, can feel the horse move away from your finger tips.

If there is no movement, or if the horse objects to being asked, it could be a red flag of soreness, atrophy, and/or arthritis. Not every horse will have a lot of movement here, but hopefully there will be some, or at least the horse will try.

This is also a good exercise to do daily to strengthen a horse's back and abdominals. Just a few times, though, as it is just as hard for an out-of-shape horse to do this as it is for an out-of-shape human to start doing daily sit-ups.

44. Tail Stretch

Because the horse's tail is an extension of his spine, the tail stretch can benefit your horse's back. Unlike most other mammals, most of the horse's spine is uniquely immobile—except for the tail. The assessment of the tail is an important one, but only if you feel it is safe to do so. If the horse is fidgety, restless, or disrespectful—or if the horse has his tail clamped between his hind legs—consider passing on this part of the assessment.

If the horse is quiet and engaged, though, a tail stretch can tell you a lot about the status of the horse's vertebrae, and the strength and soundness of his back end. You previously observed if the tail hung straight, or if it was cocked to one side or the other. Be extra gentle with any tail manipulation if the tail was carried to the left or the right, as there might be soreness that you do not want to aggravate.

Earlier, you grasped the tail about eight inches from the top and shook it gently to see if the tail, in general, was flexible. Now, gently pull the tail to the left and to the right, and note the horse's attitude. Don't pull so hard that the horse is pulled off balance. Just gentle, steady pressure.

Then try to raise the top of the tail. Ideally, the tail will have good rotational movement, top, bottom, left, and right. If there is resistance in one direction or another, there might be arthritis or muscle tightness, or the horse's spine just might be out of whack.

The last stretch is a backward one. Stand behind the horse, grasp the tail below the bone and pull outward and behind at the same angle as the croup. The horse should lean forward into this stretch while you hold it for about five seconds. The stretch decompresses the spine and temporarily adds space between the vertebrae. Only do this stretch if you feel safe, and be sure to watch the horse's entire body language so you can let go and get out of the way of any kicks. Usually, though, this stretch feels good to a horse and he or she will at least try to lean forward. If the horse takes steps to the side, or backs up to relieve the pressure, think about soreness somewhere in the spine. Soreness has been mentioned a lot and most horses, like many people, have some. It is the degree of discomfort that matters. If there is only mild soreness

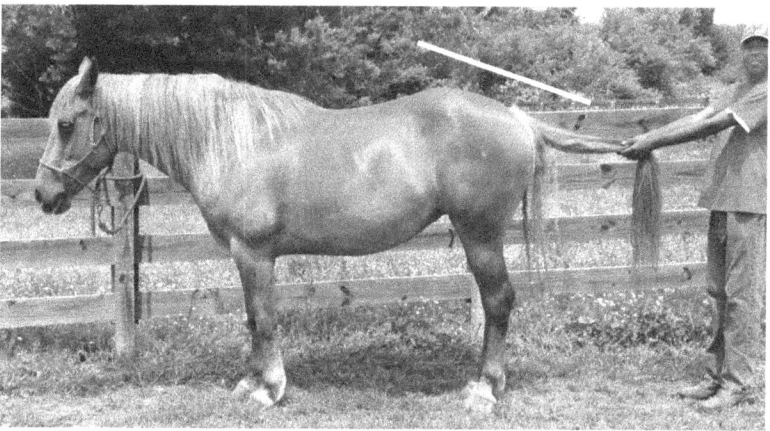

The tail should be extended to the same angle as the croup.

on the left shoulder and along the left side of the back, maybe it can be worked out with massage. If, however, the horse shows moderate to severe discomfort over a half dozen areas of his body, it complicates matters.

45. Gaits (overview)

The movement of the horse really is quite magical, and while horses all move their legs in the same pattern when they walk, trot or gait, and canter, just like people, no two horses have exactly the same movement.

The distance, or the length of the stride, is important, and will depend on the horse's breed, build, and level of physical fitness. It makes sense that a horse with long legs and a short back (think tall rectangle) will have a longer stride than a horse with a long back and short legs (long rectangle). Typically, the longer the stride the more movement the rider gets.

Length of stride and the movement it provides also ties into the height ratio of withers to hip. If the horse's hip is taller than the withers, then powerful hindquarter legs and muscles can better push the left and right sides of the rider's pelvis forward. If the hip is too much higher, though, the upward slant of the horse's back may tip the rider's upper body forward. The same problem exists in reverse if the horse's withers are significantly higher than the horse's hip. In this instance the tilt of the horse's topline could tip the rider back. As they say, balance in all things!

Remember looking at the horse's front legs? Here, you get to see how the conformation you noted on the leg translates to how the horse actually moves. There are exceptions to every rule, but in general, the horse who toed in, will "paddle," or swing his lower legs to the outside, when moving.

Years ago I showed a very toed-in Appaloosa mare in saddle-seat classes. She was reserve world champion one year, mostly, I believe, due to her big, extended trot. But, she paddled outward so badly that her hoof hit the bottom of my boot when she was in her big trot, and I ended up riding the entire season with huge bruises on the soles of my feet. Not all horses toe in this badly or will cause rider discomfort, but be sure to watch the movement of the lower front limbs when doing a gait assessment.

Horses who toe-out can also be base narrow. These horses sometimes "plait." Look for the foot and lower leg to wing inward and land in front of the other front foot. In the process, the horse sometimes hits his hoof, pastern, fetlock, or even lower cannon bone. Bell boots and splint boots can help prevent scrapes and bruising when the hoof hits the opposite leg, but won't cure the problem.

46. Backing

Your prospective horse should also be asked to back. This is where some horses refuse. It may be because the horse has not been asked to back recently, and that's not an awful thing, as it is not difficult to teach a horse to back from the ground.

If, however, the horse refuses to back because it is painful for her to do so, you might take another look at the back, lumbar vertebrae, hips, stifle, and hocks. Some people do not ask their older horses to back at all. But, the horse should try to back when asked.

The sequence the horse moves his legs in a back is that of a reverse trot. The diagonal pairs of right front and left hind should move backward together, as should the opposite diagonal of left front and right hind. If the horse is backing very slowly, you might see the right front move before the left hind, but if the horse backs with his legs out of sequence, that might be an indication of muscle atrophy or soreness.

47. The Walk

One major component of the walk to look for is the horse's ability to overtrack. Overtracking is the amount of distance the horse's back hoofprint over steps the horse's front hoof imprint at the walk. To see this, have someone lead the horse past you at a good walk. First, watch where the horse lands her front feet, then watch to see if the horse's hind feet fall short of the front imprint, land on top of it, or land in front of it. These three options are called undertracking, tracking up, and overtracking. Depending on how fast the horse is being led, some horses can do all three (just not at the same time).

The sequence of the horse's stride at the walk is left hind, left front, right hind, and right front. In this way the walk is a lateral gait. Left, left, right, right. The important consideration is how far underneath the horse reaches with her back legs. A horse who regularly overtracks should be flexible and sound. Overtracking is also very often a sign of a horse who is free of arthritis or soreness. The horse's build, however,s has to be taken into consideration. A horse with a long body and short legs may also be sound, and free of arthritis and soreness, even though it is physically impossible for her to reach underneath herself as far as a leggy Thoroughbred can.

Another consideration to look for is whether the horse tracks up evenly on the left and right sides. Tracking differently left and right is quite common in horses who have suffered an injury, or who have overused a specific joint. The result is an uneven gait for the rider. Rather than an even push left and right from the hind legs, there could be a big push from the left hind, and a medium push from the right. The horse then makes up for the shorter distance from the right hind with a larger step from the right front.

Something else to look for is if the horse's back legs follow in the same path as the front. To see this, stand behind the horse while someone leads him in a straight line away from you. Some horses who have back problems will land their back feet to the left or right of where the front feet land. Often, you can let your eye travel up to the horse's topline and see that the horse's hips and lower spine are also canted to the left or right.

While you are standing behind the horse, also look to see if the hocks wobble in or out. Wobbly hocks can be a sign of weakness in the joint, and can affect the horse's way of going and how much work he can handle.

48. The Trot

While the walk is a lateral gait, the trot is a diagonal gait. Left hind and right front move forward together, then the right hind and left front. If the horse is going fast enough and is collected enough, there may be a period of suspension between strides where all four of the horse's legs are off the ground.

Stride length also plays a factor here. Horses with a lot of knee and hock action, such as the Hackney Pony, Saddlebred, and similar breeds, will have a lot of bounce to the trot, but the stride will be shorter. Instead of length, these horses use up their motion in knee and hock height. A Thoroughbred, or even a breedy Quarter Horse will have a long, low reach to her stride. Here, withers and hip height will determine how smooth the gait is to ride. Going back to conformation, even the height the neck is carried

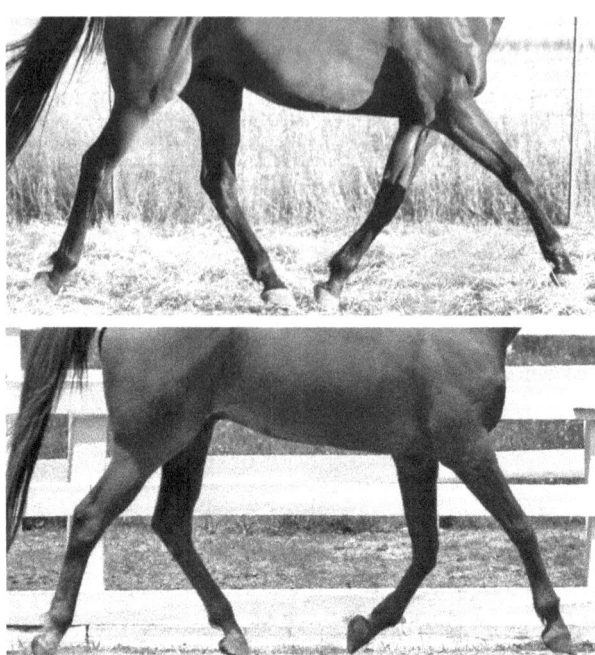

While both horses are trotting at about the same speed, it is easy to see that the horse in the top photo has a longer stride. The horse reaches farther forward with his front leg, and the distance between the front and back legs under the belly is much shorter than with the horse in the bottom photo.

will have a factor on the horse's gait. High necks indicate more knee and hock lift than a horse who carries her neck lower.

Your conformation assessment should have predicted how this horse actually moves.

49. Gaited Horses

Most gaited horses, with the exception of the Peruvian Paso, Paso Fino and one or two others, have a very long stride. Gaited horses usually overtrack well at the walk, but many gaited horses also do not gait consistently. One Tennessee Walking Horse I worked with gaited in a nice consistent manner with an experienced rider, but with a beginner or intermediate rider he sometimes trotted, sometimes paced, and at other times performed a nice running walk. This made difficult any activity that needed consistency in the gait.

50. The Canter

A strong, balanced, and even lope or canter on both the left and right lead is yet another indication of a horse whose muscles, bones, and joints are healthy. If you encounter a horse who takes one lead, but not the other, it could be he was never taught to use both leads. Or, it could be a physical sign of the dropped hip or puffy knee you discovered during your assessment.

Normally, a horse tracking clockwise will move his legs in this fashion: left rear, the diagonal pair of right rear and left front together, and then the right front as the leading leg. Some very sore horses might always travel forward with left rear and left front together, then the right rear, and then the right front. Or, have some other odd combination of a gait that resembles a canter or lope. If you have looked closely at the horse during the assessment, a funky gait such as this might not be a surprise.

Finally, does the horse canter as you expected with a normal sized stride for the height and build of the horse? Or, are the canter strides short and choppy, a possible sign of gait deviation?

51. Lameness

The fact is, a poorly conformed horse is more likely to go lame than a horse who is well put together. The terms lameness and soundness (or unsoundness) are often used interchangeably, but some people are more comfortable with a subtle difference. Depending on which person you talk to, a lameness might be recent, temporary, or something the horse is currently undergoing treatment for, while an unsoundness is a long-term, chronic condition. Others will say that a lameness is due to an injury, while an unsoundness is structural, and caused by poor conformation, poor bone structure, or weak muscles.

Regardless, if the horse you have gone to look at does not move in a rhythmic, even gait, or is obviously in pain, go back to your assessment to try to figure out why, as the "why" can often tell you if the situation can be resolved.

Soundness (or lameness) can be difficult to evaluate, and for many reasons. One, there are varying degrees of soundness. There is "perfectly sound," "serviceably sound," and "definitely lame." Perfectly sound translates to: based on the evaluation today, the horse will probably hold up for most reasonable uses. Serviceably sound means the horse will most likely be okay for some light work. Lame means just that. It is painful for the horse to move forward and there is a noticeable deviation in the gait as a result.

Another reason an unsoundness might be difficult to diagnose is if the horse is gaited, or normally has an unusual way of going, or if the horse has poor conformation, but has figured out a way to get from point A to point B that is different from other horses, but usual for this one. Whether the problem is in the shoulder, hip, hoof, hock, stifle, or any other place on the horse's body can also be tough to determine. Sometimes only a skilled diagnostician can determine the true cause of the problem, and where it is.

Should a lameness or unsoundness be a red flag for you? Quite possibly. It depends on how you expect the horse to fit into your life, the probable cause of the issue, and whether or not good care can improve matters to your expectations of the horse. Only you can decide if it is worth the risk.

Soundness is a subject where entire books have been written, so we'll only go into the most basic issues that might be seen. If, however, you suspect something is not quite right, be sure to mention it to your veterinarian and farrier (or trimmer) before the pre-purchase exams, if you are still interested in the horse.

Front-end lameness often is the easiest to see. Just as you might wince when putting a sore foot on the ground, so does your horse. Watch the horse as he is walked and trotted in a straight line on a loose lead over firm, even ground. Usually, a horse will raise his head when weight bearing on a sore front limb. Or, you might notice the horse drop his head when the sound leg hits the ground. In either case, the horse's head and neck will be higher whenever the ouchy limb becomes weight bearing. This is true either at the walk or at the trot.

Rear-end lamenesses can be harder to spot, but generally, if the lameness is in the rear, the horse will drop his hip on the side that is lame. That's why it often is easiest to spot a rear lameness by looking at the horse's hip, or rear topline, rather than at his legs.

On the off chance that the horse is unsound on both front or both rear legs, there will be little to no head or hip raising or lowering. But, the horse's stride will be short and choppy, and the horse may, understandably, be cranky or unwilling.

If you think the horse is off, look for the injury from the ground up while the horse is standing still. If he rests one leg continually, or avoids placing weight on a leg, that's a good indication the limb is sore—somewhere. You can check for heat or swelling, although you may not find either. Then pick up the hoof. Stone bruises or tender soles after a trim, or even rocky terrain, can cause a horse to be ouchy. Possibly, the horse has an abscess in his hoof. Moving up the leg and into the shoulder or hip, there can be any number of muscle strains or other injuries. It is not up to you to diagnose, but if you can get a probable cause it can help with your assessment and selection.

Sometimes the horse owner is unaware that the horse has a problem. It's best to tread lightly at first to test the owner's emotional response to the news that her horse is lame, and then suggest that a veterinarian be called. Even though you care, you do not want to offer a diagnosis or treatment, even if it comes out of concern. There may be liability issues involved if the lameness turns out to be something other than what you think, or if your suggested course of action does not improve the horse's condition.

Taking video footage of the horse as he moves can help you see exactly what, if anything, is going on. If the horse is definitely sore, do not continue the assessment. But, if the horse is promising in other ways, leave the door open with his owner and ask her to call you when the problem has been resolved.

The Final Take-Away

As a whole, these fifty-one points can seem like a great deal to look for, but with a little practice, you can learn to assess all of the attributes for an individual horse in less than ten minutes. You will develop the skill of looking at the side view of the horse and taking it all in at once: the angles of the shoulder and pasterns, levelness of withers to the top of the hip, height of the neck, tightness of the belly, look of the eye, and more.

As you go through the assessment, you can add the information you see to the information you already have about the horse: age, training, personality, temperament, size, etcetera. Soon, you will have a full picture and can make a decision as to whether or not this horse will be a valued addition to your herd.
    There is one more photo to see, and it might take a while to wrap your brain around it. In my clinics and seminars I used to introduce this photo first, before going point by point, nose to tail. But, people seemed to process it better after they had digested all of the other information first.
    It is a photo of the perfect horse. Or, as perfect as you will find. On the next page you will see a horse with perfect angles, and perfect thirds across the topline. Only this time the thirds are

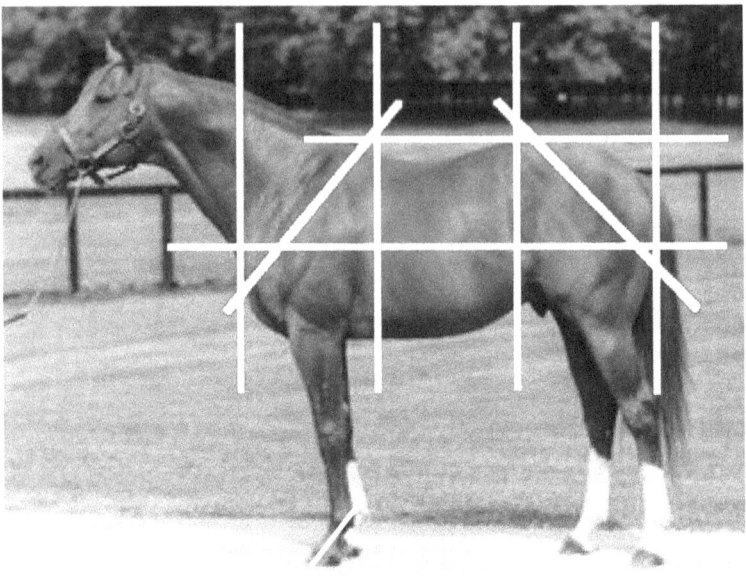

The perfect horse.

drawn a little differently: one third from point of chest to withers, one third from withers to where the underbelly ties in to the stifle, and one third from there to the point of the buttocks.

What about the original thirds: back, loin, and croup? They are there, too, and they also are in perfect proportion. So as not to get too many confusing lines in one illustration, those thirds were intentionally left out.

This horse also has matching shoulder and hip angles, and is straight across the topline from top of withers to top of hip. He is also straight across from his point of shoulder to his point of buttocks. Finally, the front pastern angle matches the angle of the front shoulder, and is a reverse of the hip angle.

Will you find a twin to this horse? Probably not. But you now have tools to make more informed decisions about the horses you do find, and about the horses who are already in your herd.

And, as the horses in your herd age, it is important to assess them annually, to be sure each is still up to the work you expect. It is hard to see our horses age, and to understand that they can no longer do what they used to, but we all want to do what is best for our horses, and this assessment will help you do just that.

After the Assessment

After you are done with the evaluation, and if you have just assessed a prospective horse rather than an existing horse in your herd, you now have enough knowledge to ask the owner more detailed questions about the horse. Until you have completed the assessment, you may not have enough data to ask for the info you need.

We are all a product of our environment and a horse is no different. An early injury, a barn fire, or a previous job pulling a hay wagon might not be on the horse owner's radar. However, during the assessment you might have seen evidence of the fire or injury, or suspected that the horse was far more experienced than the owner had indicated.

Questions such as "How did he get this scar?" or "How long has he pinned his ears when he goes into a trot?" will deepen the horse's story. If the owner says this is the first time the horse has pinned his ears (and you believe her), then he may just be overwhelmed by the assessment process and think he'd rather be back in his pasture. If this is an ongoing thing for him it may just be habit, or it may be soreness.

If you know more of the horse's history it allows you to put context to the information you learned during the assessment.

Was the pony lazy? How long has he been ridden by young children? Maybe he just needs new rules. Or, he could have arthritis.

This is your opportunity to ask the owner anything you have a question about. If the horse scored low on how far he was able to flex but did flex evenly, for example, knowing that this seventeen-year-old horse has been turned out in the pasture for the past two years gives some hope that with regular work he may become more flexible.

The Vet and Farrier Exams

If you like the new horse you have just assessed and decide you want to lease or buy, there are two more steps to take: the vet and farrier (or trimmer) exams. Both of these give critical pieces of information and should answer any lingering questions you might have about the horse.

Both the vet and farrier exams should be done as soon after the assessment as is convenient. After all, if it is determined that the horse is ouchy not due to a bad trim, but because he has navicular disease, your decision about the horse might change.

Many people do have a horse vet checked, but fewer call their farrier or trimmer in for a consultation. While a veterinarian is certainly qualified to treat a hoof and spot any red flags, a trimmer or farrier can possibly spot problems your veterinarian did not look for. During the vet exam, general health and soundness are the main things he or she will look for: teeth, hearing, vision, a full lameness check, and that ugly spot of dermatitis. If there are concerns, the veterinarian might suggest some x-rays to check for coffin bone rotation, or a scope to check for ulcers. Coffin bone rotation is an indication of founder or laminitis, and many owners do not know that this has happened to their horse. Others do, but hope you won't notice.

The farrier, on the other hand, will look at the sole of the horse's hoof and tell you if the horse might be prone to stone bruising, or abscesses. She will tell you if the hoof wall is too damaged to hold a shoe, or if the horse is already shod, if the shoes are corrective, and why. Shoeing is more costly than having a horse go barefoot, so ask your farrier or trimmer if this horse is a good barefoot candidate.

Many people agree that it is better for a horse to go barefoot, if possible, but not all can. Sometimes a horse who is barefoot has trouble because of the rough terrain or hard footing that surrounds his barn. If you have a lot of gravel or rock, then your horse might have to wear shoes. Or, if you compete or ride a lot of trails, shoes may be a regular expense associated with your horse.

As with the assessment, the recommendations you receive from your veterinarian and farrier or trimmer should be added to the overall picture of the horse. The information then, as a whole, can be used to make that final decision as to whether the horse goes home with you, or stays with her current owner.

• • •

There are many more points of conformation and a lot more to study, if you so desire. But, the information you've just read will give you a broad base of knowledge when it comes to assessing a horse. It will also help you make good decisions about which horse(s) you choose to bring into your life, and which of your existing horses you choose to keep. When all is said and done the assessment is a tool to help you make an informed decision. Based on the horse's history, you may choose to take the stiff, willing horse over the perfectly sound and flexible horse who has a pushy personality. It all goes back to your needs and expectations.

Horse Assessment Form

Appendix A (also download at LisaWysocky.com)

Horse's Registered Name:_____
Stable Name: _____
Breed: _____
Year born: _____ Color: _____
Markings: _____
Height: _____ Weight: _____
Current Owner: _____
Owner Address: _____
Owner Phone: _____
Owner Email: _____
Veterinarian: _____
Trimmer/Farrier: _____
Other: _____

Rate the Following:
0 below average / 1 average / 2 above average
Mark your score in the first space, then add any comments
1. Mouth: ____ / _____
2. Teeth: ____ / _____
3. Nostril: ____ / _____

4. Bridge of the Nose: ____ / _____
5. Forehead Whorl: ____ / _____
6. Eye: ____ / _____
7. Forehead: ____ / _____
8. Ear: ____ / _____
9. Poll: ____ / _____
10. Neck: ____ / _____
11. Chest: ____ / _____
12. Front Legs (overview): ____ / _____
13. Knees: ____ / _____
14. Cannon Bones: ____ / _____
15. Amount of Bone: ____ / _____
16. Pastern and Fetlock: ____ / _____
17. Hoof: ____ / _____
18. Shoulder: ____ / _____
19. Profile: ____ / _____
20. Withers: ____ / _____
21. Posture: ____ / _____
22. Barrel: ____ / _____
23. Stomach: ____ / _____
24. Back: ____ / _____
25. Loin: ____ / _____
26. Croup: ____ / _____
27. Rear legs (overview): ____ / _____
28. Hip: ____ / _____
29. Stifle: ____ / _____
30. Hock: ____ / _____
31. Rear Pasterns: ____ / _____
32. Tail: ____ / _____
33. Muscle Tone: ____ / _____
34. Scars and Blemishes: ____ / _____

35. Skin and Hair: _____ / _____
36. Weight: _____ / _____
37. Size and Build: _____ / _____
38. Range of Motion (overview): _____ / _____
39. Head and Neck Stretch: _____ / _____
40. Nose to Chest Stretch: _____ / _____
41. Front Leg Stretch: _____ / _____
42. Back Leg Stretch: _____ / _____
43. Belly Lift: _____ / _____
44. Tail Stretch: _____ / _____
45. Gaits (overview): _____ / _____
46. Backing: _____ / _____
47. The Walk: _____ / _____
48. The Trot: _____ / _____
49. Gaited Horses: _____ / _____
50. The Canter: _____ / _____
51. Lameness: _____ / _____

Total score: _____ / 102

Additional comments:

_____
_____
_____
_____
_____
_____
_____
_____
_____
_____

The Ten-Minute Assessment

Appendix B

This quick, ten-minute assessment will help you quickly evaluate horses who might end up in your barn. It will take some time, but with enough practice you can learn to spot and evaluate many of the items below very quickly.

Shape of the Horse's Body—is the body, square, tall, or rectangular? Different body shapes give different movement, and long, rectangular horses have long backs, which can limit the amount of weight the horse carries. Are the withers and hips level, or is one higher than the other?

Nostrils—big nostrils allow the horse to bring in more air to regulate body temperature and inhale scent.

Eyes Set Wide—horses who have eyes set widely have a better range of vision and, as a whole, tend to be less spooky.

Whorl—this old superstition may have merit! What direction the whorl(s) on the forehead go, where they are, and the number of them may predict a horse's personality.

Neck Bend—can the horse flex his or her nose back to the girth area? Is flexion equal on both sides? Limited or unequal flexion can be a sign of arthritis or needed chiropractic work.

Front Legs—can you drop a straight line from chest to hoof? Crooked legs can indicate a propensity to lameness.

Hooves—hard, chipped, or shelly? If you need the horse to wear a shoe, will one stay on?

Cecal Swing—does the horse's barrel bulge more on the right side than the left?

Flank Touch—does the horse move his or her hips away when you touch the flank area? Is the movement even on the left and right sides? No movement can indicate soreness or arthritis, or a very dominant horse.

Hips Level—are the horse's hips level when the horse is standing square? Uneven hips can mean arthritis, chronic unsoundness, or that chiropractic work is needed.

Tail Centered—does the horse carry the top part of his or her tail centered between the butt cheeks? A tail carried to the left or right can mean general soreness, or even serious lower back or hip problems.

General Soreness—when you turn your fingers into a claw shape and run your hands over the horse's body, does the horse pin his or her ears? If so, the horse could be bad tempered, or have a lot of soreness.

Travels Evenly—when you watch the horse walk, does he or she track evenly front to back and left to right? If not, arthritis or chronic discomfort might be an issue.

Tracks Up or Over—does the horse track up or overtrack at a good, working walk? Does she do this evenly on both the left and right sides?

Soundness—does the horse show any signs of lameness at the walk or trot?

Parts of the Horse

Appendix C

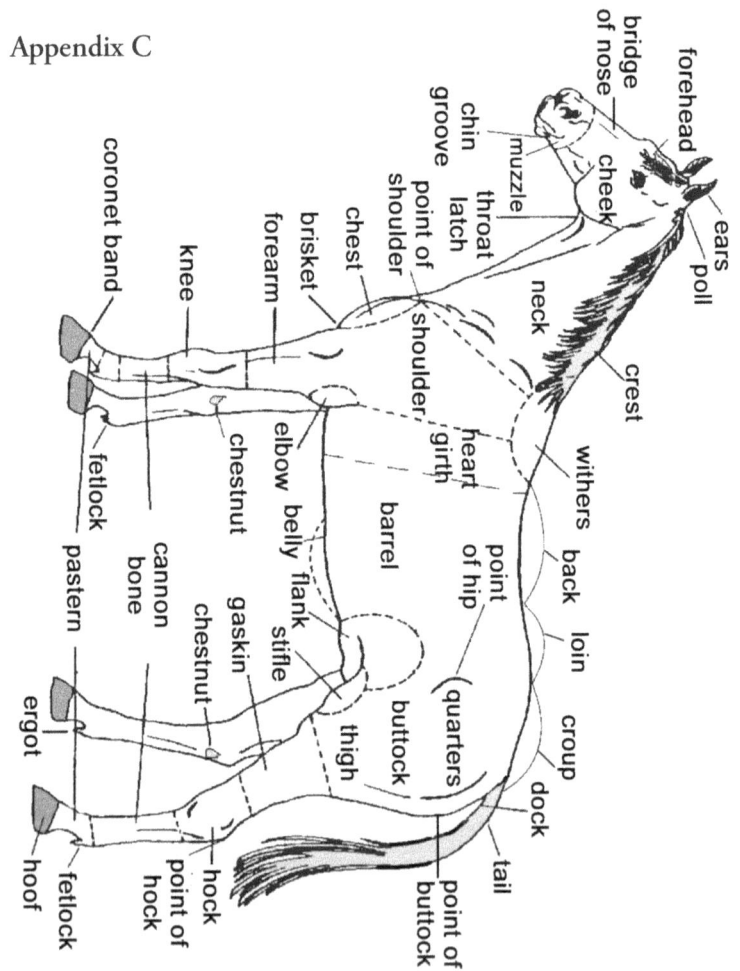

Glossary

Appendix D

The following terms are used to describe various aspects of horses. While many more terms could have been included, this glossary has been limited to those terms that might come into play when assessing a horse's conformation. In some cases, a word has several meanings, but only those meanings most relevant to the horse selection process have been included.

Some terms are quite basic, but are included for those readers who are new to horses, or to further explain the use of the word in this book.

Action:	The way a horse elevates his or her legs, knees, hocks, and feet.
Aged Horse:	An older horse. Sometimes referred to a horse with a "smooth mouth." In horse racing and in some horse shows, an aged horse is one over four years of age.
Ankle:	Incorrect term for the fetlock joint, as the hock closely corresponds to the human ankle.

Barefoot: When a horse does not wear shoes.

Blowing: A sound made by a horse who sharply exhales through flared nostrils. A horse might blow when curious, meeting another horse, or shying away from an object.

Bone: Used to describe the quality of the horse's skeletal structure. Also refers to the size and density of bone of the lower leg, which helps determine the amount of weight the horse can carry.

Bowed Tendon: An enlarged tendon along the back of the cannon bone that often is caused by heavy work.

Breedy: A horse who conforms to breed type. Also used to describe horses of thinner build, such as a Thoroughbred or Arabian.

By: The relationship of a horse to her sire in the context of pedigree. A foal is "by" her sire and "out of" her dam.

Cannon Bone: The third metacarpal or metatarsal bone of the lower leg. Sometimes called the shin bone, but it is actually comparable to bones in the human palm or foot. In horses, it is a large bone and provides support for the body weight of the horse.

Canter: A three-beat gait. In western disciplines, the canter is known as a lope. The order in which the feet hit the ground varies depending on which front leg leads, but the gait begins with the outside hind, followed by both the inside hind and outside front together, then the inside front. There is a moment during a canter when all four hooves are off the ground, known as the moment of suspension.

Capped Elbow: A swelling of the bursa caused by injury.

Capped Hock: *See Capped Elbow.*

Carriage: The way a horse carries himself, especially in the positioning of his head and neck.

Chestnuts: A callus on the inner side of the leg above the knee on the foreleg, and below the hock on the hind leg. Chestnuts vary in size and shape and are sometimes compared to human fingerprints. For purposes of identification, some breed registries require photographs of a horse's chestnuts, among other individual characteristics.

Chrome: Slang for eye-catching white markings on a horse, usually a blaze and/or stockings or socks. Also refers to flashy Paint, Pinto, or Appaloosa markings.

Clean: Legs with no blemishes; a narrow throatlatch.

Conformation: The shape and proportion of a horse's body.

Contracted Heels: A common hoof ailment, contracted heels are a narrowing of the heel between the bulbs (the soft, fleshy area where the hoof wall, heel, and coronary band come together at the back of the foot), possibly causing lameness.

Coronary Band (Coronet Band): The ring of soft tissue just above the hoof that blends into the skin of the leg.

Coupling:	It includes the bottom of the middle phalanx bone.
	The sunken area below the lumbar vertebrae, behind the last rib and in front of the point of the hip. Ideally, it should be as short as possible.
Crest:	The center of the top of the horse's neck.
Cribbing:	A vice where the horse grabs the edge of an object, such as a fence board, with his front teeth and arches his neck. More severe cases also suck air in simultaneously, and this is called windsucking.
Croup:	The croup runs from the loin to the tail, and from the point of the hip to the point of the buttock. One of the "thirds" that include the back and loin.
Curb:	Several types of lameness that include a swelling on the back of the lower leg. Also, any number of soft tissue injuries of the hock area.
Dock:	The muscular portion of a horse's tail, where the hair is rooted. Sometimes refers only to the upper portion of this area, where the tail attaches to the hindquarters. Also, to cut a horse's tail at the dock, seen most often on carriage and draft horses to keep their tails from becoming caught in the harness.
Draft Horse:	Generic term for many breeds of large, muscular, heavy horses developed primarily as farm or harness horses who plow fields, pull

	wagons, log timber, and similar heavy, pulling work, versus "light," or riding horses.
Easy Keeper:	A horse who needs little food to maintain condition, and who may be prone to obesity.
Equine:	Any member of the genus Equus.
Equus:	The genus that includes the horse, donkey, zebra and all other surviving members of the Equidae family.
Ergot:	A small callus on the back of the fetlock, often concealed by hair and thought to be a remnant of the pad of the prehistoric toe.
Farrier:	A professional hoof care specialist who does hoof trimming, and who also uses blacksmithing skills to do horse shoeing.
Feathers:	Long hair on the fetlocks of horses. Most horses have some feather, but in draft breeds it may cover the feet and even extend up the back of the legs.
Fetlock:	The joint above the pastern. It is equivalent to the base joint of a human finger or toe.
Filly:	A young female horse, normally one under four years of age.
Flank:	The profile side of a horse's upper back leg.
Founder:	The most severe form of laminitis, an inflammatory condition that affects the laminae of the hoof. The third phalanx (the coffin bone) rotates, often becomes deformed, and in severe cases, may puncture the bottom surface of the hoof. It is a leading cause of death

among horses, especially in breeds that are easy keepers.

Frog: The tough, rubbery, triangular part of the underside of a horse hoof that acts as a shock absorber for the foot and assists in blood circulation of the lower leg.

Gait: The sequence in which a horse moves her legs. Gaits are divided into natural gaits (those performed by most horses), and those that are either trained by humans, or are specific to a few breeds. The natural gaits are walk, trot, canter/lope, and gallop. Other gaits include the pace, and ambling gaits such as the rack and running walk.

Gaited Horse: A horse who performs a gait other than, or in addition to, the trot. Many breeds are considered gaited, including the Peruvian Paso, Paso Fino, some Saddlebreds, the Missouri Fox Trotter, and Tennessee Walking Horse.

Gallop: The fastest natural horse gait. Like the canter or lope, there is a moment during a gallop when all four hooves are off the ground, known as the moment of suspension. At fastest speeds, the gallop differs from the canter in that it becomes an irregular four beat gait, rather than a three-beat gait. At the gallop, the second beat of the canter—when diagonal front and hind legs strike the ground together—is broken into two beats in quick succession.

Goosey:	Jumpy.
Grade:	A horse who has only a small amount of recognizable breeding, or none at all. Generally unregistered and unregisterable.
Hand:	A measurement of the height of a horse. Originally taken from the size of a grown man's hand but now standardized to four inches. The measurement is taken from the ground to the withers. It is expressed with a number, a period and a second number. 15.3 hands would be fifteen times four inches, plus three inches—or 63 inches.
Hard Keeper:	A horse who needs a large amount of food to maintain condition.
Head Shy:	A horse who is hesitant to have his head touched or handled.
Heavy:	A draft horse is often called a heavy horse.
Hinny:	The offspring of a female donkey and a male horse. The reverse parentage (with somewhat different appearance and characteristics) is a mule.
Hock:	A joint of the horse's hind leg, midway between the horse's body and the ground. The hock corresponds to the ankle and heel of the human.
Jack:	An uncastrated male donkey or ass.
Jennet:	A small, gaited horse developed in Spain, used for riding. Or, a female donkey.
Jenny:	A female donkey, sometimes called a jennet.

Jog: A slow trot.

Knee: The joint of a horse's front leg between the cannon bone and the forearm. It is equivalent to the human wrist.

Laminitis: Inflammation of the laminae of the hoof, and possibly linked to metabolic disorder, obesity, or ingestion of excess starches or sugars. Laminitis can cause lameness and severe pain.

Lead: The leading front leg of the horse at the lope or canter, and gallop. On a curve, a horse usually leads with the inside leg. Also a lead rope: a line or rope attached to a halter to lead a horse from one place to another.

Lope: A form of slow canter seen in western-style riding.

Markings: The white markings on the horse's face, legs, and the odd body spot on an otherwise solid-colored horse.

Mule: The long-eared offspring of a male donkey and a horse mare. Mules are almost always sterile. The reverse parentage (with somewhat different appearance and characteristics) is a hinny.

Near side: The left side of a horse, which is the traditional side where most activities around a horse take place.

Off: A term to describe when a horse is lame or unsound.

Off Side: The right side of a horse.

Out of:	The relationship of a horse to his dam in the context of pedigree. A foal is "by" his sire and "out of" or from his dam.
Pace:	A two-beat, lateral gait where the front and hind legs on the same side move forward at the same time.
Parrot Mouth:	A malformation of the jaw where the upper front teeth protrude beyond the lower jaw. A severe parrot mouth could make chewing difficult for the horse.
Pastern:	The part of the leg between the fetlock and the coronary band.
Pointing:	Resting a foreleg in indication of soreness in that leg or foot.
Poll:	The bump just behind the ears.
Pony:	In general, small horses that typically mature shorter than 14.2 hands, or 58 inches.
Proprioception:	The innate knowing of the relative position of each body part.
Purebred:	An animal with documented parentage recognized by a breed registry and free of breeding from lines outside those of the breed in question. Not to be confused with Thoroughbred, which is a specific breed of horse.
Smooth Mouth:	An older horse who has worn the indentations or "cups" from his incisors, which usually occurs about the age of eight.
Sound:	Terminology to describe a healthy horse.

Splint: Ossification of small bones on the inside of the cannon bone. Splints are hard bumps that can form after trauma. An unsoundness when newly injured, a splint may mature into a blemish with no effect on soundness.

Sport Horse: General term for a horse bred and/or trained for eventing, dressage, or jumping. May also include hunters and horses trained for combined driving.

Stock Horse: A horse who herds livestock, or is trained for reining, roping, or cutting; a generic term for horse breeds developed for handling cattle. The term is also used to describe the Appaloosa, Quarter Horse, and Paint breeds.

Stocky: A squat horse with bunchy muscles.

Stride: The distance from the imprint of a forefoot until the same foot hits the ground again; the sequence of footfalls in a specific gait.

Stringhalt: A disorder that causes a jerking movement when walking, and a higher than natural movement of one or both hind legs.

Substance: Assessment of the overall muscularity of a horse, the width and depth of the body, and the quality of bone.

Thrush: A common bacterial infection in the hoof, specifically in the area of the frog.

Topline: The line from the poll to the dock of the tail; or on a pedigree chart, the paternal side, which is found on the top of the chart.

Trimmer:	A person who trims horse's feet, but who does not shoe horses.
Typey:	Slang for a horse who conforms to his breed standards, or type.
Unsound:	A horse with significant lameness or other health problems.
Warmblood:	A descriptive word for many middle-weight sport horse breeds. Most originated in Europe by crossbreeding draft horses with light breeds such as Thoroughbreds or Arabians. "Warm" refers to the cross of a cold-blood and a hot-blood. It does not relate to body temperature.
White Line:	The junction between hoof wall and sole on the bottom of the horse's hoof. White Line Disease is a widening of the white line, or a separation of the hoof wall from the sole. It is caused by bacteria, fungi, or both.
Whorl:	A circular arrangement of hairs, usually on a horse's forehead, neck, or chest. Their location is one means of horse identification, and may predict personality.
Wind Puff:	A puffy bump filled with excess synovial fluid, and usually seen on the fetlock joint. Also sometimes seen on the knee. Wind puffs are caused by injury or overuse, but rarely cause lameness.

Acknowledgements

When I started this book I had so much information to share that I was not sure how to include it all. One thought about gait, for instance, led me to the structure of bones in the horse's knee, and then to typical knee action in different breeds, and then to how knee action affects the rider. My enthusiasm was so great that I had to rein myself in.

The result is, hopefully, only information that involves conformation points that will help you assess horses that you either currently own or are thinking of adding to your herd. The rest will have to wait for another day, and another book. I hope you will consider this book as a jumping off point to learn more about specific areas of horses that interest you.

Many thanks to Quincy and Tessie, two horses who are perfect in their imperfection, and who posed for most of the photographs. Quincy is a 16.0-hand, solid colored Appaloosa gelding (registered name Request for Success); and Tessie is a 15.2-hand, Belgian/Quarter Horse mare.

Also included are Braxton (registered name Hard to Handle), a 16.2-hand off-the-track Thoroughbred; and Lex, a 16.2-hand Thoroughbred/Belgian/Shire cross. All four are therapy horses at Colby's Army in Ashland City, Tennessee.

Other horses include Gunner, a Tennessee Walking Horse; Baby, a lovely, large gaited pony who has since gone on to greener pastures; and Snoqualmie (registered name Snowy Moon), a 14.2-hand Appaloosa mare who has also crossed the rainbow bridge.

Thanks also to Kylan Jenkins, who appears in a few of the photos. And to you, the reader: huge thanks for your interest. Every bit we learn about horses enriches our experience with them. I hope *Essential Horse Conformation* added something to your base of knowledge.

If you have questions, I will do my best to answer them. I hope you will email me at lisainfo@comcast.net, or visit me online at LisaWysocky.com.

Photo Credits:

All photos by Lisa Wysocky.

www.ingramcontent.com/pod-product-compliance
Lightning Source LLC
Chambersburg PA
CBHW070449050426
42451CB00015B/3406